THE LAST
GERMAN EMPRESS

THE LAST
GERMAN EMPRESS

Empress Augusta Victoria,
Consort of Emperor William II

John Van der Kiste

A & F

First published by Amazon KDP 2014
Revised and expanded edition published by A & F 2015

A & F Publications
South Brent, Devon, England, UK

ISBN-13:978-1511613965
ISBN-10:1511613963

Typeset 11pt Roman
Printed by Createspace

Contents

Preface

Augusta Victoria, the third and last German Empress ('Dona' in the family), is one of the less-remembered personalities of imperial Germany. Over the last century or so many biographers have focused on her husband, Emperor William II, his parents, Emperor Frederick III and Empress Victoria, who was known as Empress Frederick during her widowhood, and to a lesser extent his paternal grandparents Emperor William I and Empress Augusta. Yet an examination of existing sources reveals very little about her in German, and not one volume in English.

Once referred to by Queen Victoria in a moment of exasperation as a 'poor little insignificant Princess', she was never noted for her intellectual or political gifts, or indeed any exceptional qualities. Beside her mother-in-law and her late nineteenth-century contemporary Elisabeth, Empress of Austria, she has always cut a less interesting figure. By inclination she was never a dominant personality. Even so, changing circumstances, particularly those relating to the character of her mercurial husband, eventually prevailed on her to take a more supportive, even occasionally assertive, role in the last few years of the German Empire.

After having previously written about several other members of the Hohenzollern dynasty, I have relished the challenge of looking at the life of one of the more important and at the same time comparatively neglected figures.

I would like to thank Sue Woolmans for her invaluable help, advice and regular supply of illustrations and other useful relevant material, Sylvia Hemsil for her excellent proofreading, and my wife Kim for her checking through the manuscript and her encouragement throughout. At the same time I must acknowledge the support and interest of several fellow royal devotees on Facebook and elsewhere for their interest and support.

- 1 -

Early life, 1858-80

On 11 September 1856 Frederick, the eldest son of Christian Augustus II, Duke of Schleswig-Holstein-Sonderburg-Augustenburg, married Adelaide, the second daughter of Ernest Christian Charles IV, Duke of Hohenlohe-Langenburg and Feodora of Leiningen, the elder half-sister of Queen Victoria. Within the next two decades there would be seven children of the marriage. The first was Frederick William, born on 3 August 1857 at Dolzig Castle near Frankfurt. The second, born on 22 October 1858, was given the names Augusta Victoria Frederica Louise Feodora Jenny, though she was generally known by the family nickname, Dona.

All too soon the happy home, which had been celebrating a new arrival in the family, was to become one of mourning. When she was just one week old her brother died after a short illness at the age of fourteen months, and for over a year she was the only occupant of the nursery. In January 1860 her mother gave birth to a second daughter, Caroline Matilda. Nicknamed Calma, she would always be the prettiest of the girls, and partly because of their closeness in age her elder sister's favourite. Two years later to the same week a second brother Gerhard was born. He was another sickly infant, who only survived for eleven weeks. The fifth child, Ernst Gunther, a healthy son and heir at last, appeared in August 1863, followed by two more sisters, Louise Sophie in April 1866, and Feodora Adelaide, the youngest, in July 1874.

When Augusta Victoria was three months old William, the eldest child of Prince and Princess Frederick William of Prussia and third in line to the throne, was born in Berlin. The parents of both children were close friends, and the youngsters often played happily together. It would later become evident that even at this early stage some of the previous generation began to foresee that both children, so close in age to one another, might make ideal partners in the future.

5

However it was the ascendancy of Prussia which would cause such unhappiness for the family and their standing in Germany, yet ironically in doing so would later hold out one of the richest prizes possible for the eldest child. When King Frederick VII of Denmark died in November 1863 his successor, who ascended the throne as King Christian IX, claimed ownership of the duchies of Schleswig and Holstein, or the Elbe duchies, on the south of the Danish border and on the northern border of Germany. For the most part, those who lived in the duchies merely wanted independence, under a prince of their own choice. Public opinion looked to Frederick to assert his rights as their ruler. The government of Prussia, under the rule of its Minister-President, Otto von Bismarck, intended to claim and absorb these territories into the German Confederation.

War was declared in January 1864, and within a matter of weeks Denmark was defeated. Bismarck soon made it plain that Prussia had no intention of recognising 'Fritz Holstein', who was now thus in the anomalous position of being a Duke without a duchy. As a result there would always be a lingering feeling of resentment of the house of Hohenzollern on the part of the unfortunate Augustenbergs.

Although he was depressed as well as dispossessed, Frederick managed to find a great source of comfort in his family life, and in particular the love and companionship of his surviving children. Augusta Victoria, who would always be known in the family as Dona, was reckoned to be his favourite. In appearance she was slim and rather plain as a small girl, and the elder generation compared her unfavourably with her younger sister Caroline Matilda, who was said to be more musical and with a more lively personality as well as blessed with prettier looks. Among those who had praise for both sisters was the woman destined to become her mother-in-law, the German Crown Princess Frederick William. 'It is strange how good some children are – and how little trouble they give,' she wrote to her mother, Queen Victoria, when Augusta Victoria was nine years old. 'Ada's children are patterns of obedience, gentleness – the best of dispositions'.[1]

The Duchess seemed less able to manage with their reversal of fate and fortune, and the loss of prestige it implied, than her more philosophical husband. A combination of the birth of her daughter Louise Sophie, and the end of her husband's hopes of being a Duke in anything more than name, had a dire effect on her personality. She became increasingly moody and difficult, withdrawing into herself and subject to severe depression. An increasing gulf formed between her and her children, who subsequently drew much closer to their father. Interestingly, in the years to come, her eldest daughter would similarly find it difficult to reconcile herself to a loss of status, and in her case a far more pronounced one, after having been the first lady of the German Empire for thirty years.

At this time Crown Prince and Princess Frederick William were not only great friends of the Augustenburg family, but also anxious to do what they could to try and advance their status. The Crown Princess had already championed the merits of the Duke's younger brother Christian, an easygoing and thoroughly likeable if not particularly distinguished or good-looking prince, and it was partly due to this that in 1865 he was introduced to her sister Helena, whom he married in July 1866. Despite the age difference of fifteen years between bride and bridegroom, it would prove to be one of the happiest and least troubled marriages among the children of Queen Victoria. Resentment of the victorious Prussians as a state had run high in the English royal family since Bismarck's wars against Denmark and then Austria, but except in the case of the ardently pro-Danish Prince and Princess of Wales (the latter being a Danish princess), it made little difference to their friendship with members of the Prussian royal family. Now the Crown Princess had in mind the possibility that her eldest son William, still only a boy, might in time become the husband of one of the daughters of the wronged Duke.

As the girls grew up, they were taught by a French-Swiss governess, and then later by an Englishwoman, Miss Walker. It was partly at her father's insistence that as a child Augusta Victoria became fluent in English and Danish as well as German. Whether they were sitting through Bible lessons with the ducal chaplain, or playing in the nursery, discipline was the watchword, and all the children were brought up to be reserved, submissive, and obedient. On the rare occasions that Dona misbehaved, the governess would invoke the name of Bismarck, the great bogey, to scare her into obedience. The fear that the monster who had always been the family's great enemy might suddenly burst through the door was enough make her become as good as gold again.

In March 1869, two years to the day after the death of his wife, her paternal grandfather, Duke Christian Augustus II, also died. He and the Duchess had hardly ever left their estate, Primkenau Castle, in Silesia, where they moved after the war in 1866. Duke Frederick now inherited the estate and they sold Dolzig Palace, in order to facilitate their move to Primkenau. In July 1870, during their first summer there, the Franco-Prussian war broke out. His friend, Crown Prince Frederick William of Prussia, invited Duke Frederick to serve in the military forces of the North German Confederation.

Whatever his personal views about Bismarck and his methods may have been, he was a loyal German and Hohenzollern first and foremost, and always ready to take up arms on behalf of the shortly-to-be-united confederation against the traditional enemy, France. Within six months the latter was defeated, Emperor Napoleon III abdicated, and a French republic was proclaimed. On the ashes of one empire, in the Salle des Glaces at Versailles, another – the German Reich – was proclaimed, under the leadership of Prussia and the figurehead of the arch-conservative, rather grumpy Emperor William I. As a concession to the sensibilities of the other German kingdoms and duchies, he was styled German Emperor, in preference to Emperor of Germany.

● ● ● ● ●

At the age of twelve, Augusta Victoria was developing into a slender if rather short girl, with thick golden hair and a smooth complexion. Although the family and close observers sometimes commented on her round and pudgy cheeks, and the fact that she was definitely no beauty, she was judged by all to have a graceful manner and queenly bearing. She had some artistic ability, was good at sketching and drawing, liked music and was interested in history, but she was not especially fond of reading and could never be considered particularly intellectual or clever. Like other princesses of her time she had been taught the arts of sewing, knitting and crochet. Determined that his children should grow up fit, healthy and used to exercise, their father had insisted on a fairly demanding regime for her and Caroline Matilda, including long walks in the forests near Primkenau Castle in all weathers.

Finance had always been an issue for the family, as it was expensive for them to maintain a large castle and the grounds that went with it. When the family needed to travel they could not afford a formal carriage, and the Duke was obliged to hire a local farmer who would chauffeur them in a hand-drawn wooden cart, which was generally pulled by a mule or even a cow. Although money was in short supply, they always felt a personal obligation to try and improve the quality of life for the peasants who lived around their estate.

When they arrived at Primkenau, the level of poverty was high, and in order to help those who were worst off, the Duke provided additional jobs on the family estate, as well as donating sums of money for the ducal chaplain to help the needy who lived nearby. As a child Augusta Victoria was regularly given small sums of pocket money which she would save up, so that generous amounts could be distributed by the pastors every Christmas. From time to time she and her sisters went out with the chaplain so they could all hand it out together and tend to the needs of the people at the same time, going into the countryside on foot, taking presents and medicines as well. One day she and her sister were walking in the country lanes, when they saw an elderly woman making a tremendous effort to drag a cart up the hill which was clearly too heavy for her on her own. At once they ran to her assistance so they could do the job for her.

In the summer of 1875 Augusta Victoria and Caroline Matilda were confirmed together in the Evangelical Lutheran Church. The ceremony was presided over by Pastor Meissner, and attended by the Duke, Duchess, their family and household. Now her parents decided that it was time for the elder daughter to broaden her education and make an appearance at some of the more well-connected courts. Such trips were generally financed by their relations in Coburg, Baden and Carlsruhe. Once she paid a visit to the south of France, which despite its newly-acquired republican status had recently become a popular vacation centre for European royalty. However the French Mediterranean did not evoke any response in her, and in later life she would always have a particular antipathy to the country.

From time to time she went to England in order to visit her paternal uncle Christian, the husband of Queen Victoria's third daughter Helena. They and their family, two sons and two daughters, lived together at Cumberland Lodge in Windsor Great Park, close to the Queen. As the years went by Augusta Victoria would foster an increasing dislike of most of the British royal family, but she would always treasure her close ties with her uncle and aunt Christian.

● ● ● ● ●

The Holstein princesses were now considered ready for the consideration of young bachelor princes, and their parents, who might be looking for a suitable bride. It was during one of these visits to England that she came face to face with her distant Prussian cousin William. They had previously met briefly in 1868, when the Holsteins visited the Crown Prince and Princess at Potsdam, but only now, on the threshold of adult life, were they were really struck with each other.

At the age of nineteen, Prince William of Prussia had formed something of an attachment to his cousin Elizabeth of Hesse, but she did not show any reciprocal affection for him, although he persisted for a while. Immediately after he had returned from a visit to his cousins at Darmstadt in April 1878, his mother wrote to tell him that she had heard much about his other female cousins – at Holstein. Augusta Victoria, she said, was the favourite of his uncle Christian and aunt Helena, '& they also think her the prettiest which I fancy you do also! They are most dear girls, - & their like, is not easily to be found.'[2]

Within a few weeks, he was complaining to Elizabeth's mother, his aunt Alice, Grand Duchess of Hesse, that his mother was trying to force him out of any ideas of marriage with her, and into one with Dona, against his will. Alice did not hesitate to make sure that other members of the family knew how annoyed he was with his mother, a tactless move which resulted in fierce disputes between mother and son in the summer. In later life he would say that he believed his mother and grandmother between them had decided on such a match while he was still a child.[3] (Coincidentally, Queen Victoria herself always knew that the marriage between herself and her cousin Prince Albert had been as good as decided by the elder generation of the family while they were still very young, especially by their uncle Leopold, first King of the Belgians. By a further coincidence, this was another union in which the bride was three months older than the groom).

The Crown Princess was 'in despair', having been almost certain that a marriage between William and her Holstein niece was almost inevitable. Early in June she wrote to Helena that since his journeys to Darmstadt, he had completely changed his mind, and 'he felt himself too young for his Cousins of Holstein!' Alice, she was sure, had 'quite turned Willie's head (not on purpose I am sure)'.[4]

Nevertheless, on 30 August Frederick and Adelaide and their two eldest daughters visited Potsdam. This may or may not have been at the express invitation of the Crown Princess and Helena, as a final attempt to bring William and Augusta Victoria together. If it was, it achieved its objective. The Crown Prince noted rather cautiously in his diary that 'Victoria seems to make an impression on Wilhelm'.[5] From this point onwards, it seemed to the family that 'Dona' was the only one whom he had ever loved, and Ella was completely forgotten. Ella later married Grand Duke Serge of Russia, but their marriage was to be childless. Two of her younger sisters, Irene and Alexandra, gave birth to haemophiliac sons, the latter as Empress of Russia with disastrous consequences for her son and heir, Alexis, and indeed for the Romanov dynasty. If Ella was also a carrier of haemophilia, then William might well have had a fortunate escape.

In April 1879 he was on a hunting trip at Görlitz, not far from Primkenau, when he received an invitation from her father to join him on a pheasant hunt. On his parents' acceptance he went, and the story is told that one afternoon when he was exploring the grounds around the castle, he came upon Augusta Victoria, resting in a hammock tied between two rose garland firs. The sight apparently awakened something in him. That he should have fallen in love with such a vision may seem a little far-fetched, and the tale may well owe something to somebody's romantic imagination, but in spite of this he had long aware that his parents would eagerly approve of such a marriage. He proposed to her, and she immediately accepted him. As a formal marriage settlement still had to be arranged, it was not publicly announced right away.

When members of the immediate family were told, most of them were surprised that he had not fallen for her sister Caroline Matilda instead. The Crown Prince was particularly taken aback, observing that 'his sudden changing of the saddle from the one for whom he had already declared himself to the other, who is now the "only one he has ever loved", has occurred with sudden rapidity'.[6] Moreover, the Augustenburgs were regarded as rather inferior among German princely families. There was an additional disadvantage in that, after the Duke's claim to the duchies of Schleswig and Holstein had been firmly rebuffed by Bismarck some years before, they were comparatively poor. As a result, they would be unable to make a significant contribution to the marriage dowry. However William's mind was made up, and in April 1879 he wrote to the Duke that his daughter 'has so delighted me and carried me away with her whole being and her nature that I immediately resolved with great clarity and firmness to devote all my efforts to fighting for her hand.'[7]

His delighted parents hoped that a wife's influence would soften his increasingly arrogant manner. The Crown Prince was particularly pleased at what he saw as a love match as his own marriage had been, rather than one dictated by diplomacy. Dona, he considered, was a princess 'distinguished by gifts of mind, heart and temperament as well as by dignified grace.'[8] The Crown Princess was also glad, though her joy was tempered by reservations. She thought that her eldest son was too immature to be married just yet, and thought that he had too little interest in anything except for his military career. She would have preferred to see him broaden his mind first by a little more travel, as her oldest brother, the Prince of Wales, had done before an admittedly early marriage. Moreover, she recognised that Dona's intellectual powers were very limited, and she was therefore in no position to be able to stimulate those of her husband-to-be. Nevertheless, she was of excellent character, which would go some way to compensate for her other shortcomings.

He now became very attentive to Augusta Victoria, and his mother was delighted to see how besotted he was with her. In the summer of 1879 the Crown Princess wrote to the Queen that her son was 'quite wild' about the girl whom she considered 'most charming'. She could not help comparing the sisters, saying that Dona's 'figure is much prettier than her face, but her voice and walk and manner have something very sympathetic and agreeable and graceful which Calma is not though her head is decidedly the prettier of the two.'[9]

Even so, as yet there was no formal engagement, and no immediate prospect of one taking place. Emperor William, who doted on his grandson, was initially opposed to the idea of an Augustenburg as a future Empress. At first he saw the affair as a plot which had been instigated by his daughter-in-law. Like her, he believed that his grandson was as yet too immature for marriage. Moreover, Augusta Victoria was not of equal rank; her mother's lineage was only marginally royal, and her father's family was not particularly wealthy.

A further complication had arisen regarding her father, who was not in the best of health. 'Fritz Holstein' feared that the price of the engagement for him would be an embarrassing surrender of the sovereign rights that he had never renounced. Her mother was violently opposed to the alliance, and was beginning to show signs of the increasing mental instability which would cloud her last years. Baron Stockmar told the Crown Princess that every day, there were 'unpleasant scenes which the young lady rides out with exemplary grace and submissiveness'.[10]

With winter came an apparent cooling of feelings on William's side. Moreover the Duke's health deteriorated, cancer was diagnosed, and in January 1880 he died at the early age of fifty. The Crown Princess mourned the sudden loss of a good friend, as well as the fact that he had died 'before his dear child's fate is decided'. By this time she considered the engagement was almost a certainty, and she vowed that 'if we ever do have the happiness of possessing his dear daughter in our family, there is nothing I would not do to be a comfort and a help to her.'[11]

William, it was noted, went dancing the next day. Crown Prince Frederick William attended the Duke's funeral at Primkenau, which was made worse by the grief-stricken and evidently deranged widow crying out loudly during the funeral oration at the service. He was shocked that William neither showed any evidence of emotion over his death, nor made an effort to send his condolences to his future wife over the loss of her father. When he spoke to his son about this, the latter said that as he was not betrothed to the princess, it would not look right for him to appear too involved.

In fact he had been temporarily distracted by the attentions of a mistress, and it seemed that he did not recall his 'only love' until the end of the month, when Emperor William gave formal permission for the engagement to take place. He had suspected that Bismarck, of whom he was sometimes inclined to be a little afraid, would not hear of it, but the politician was indifferent to the princess whom he dismissed as 'the cow from Holstein'. He had gathered that the girl was the gentle, submissive kind who would probably make a far more pliable Empress than Crown Princess Frederick William was ever likely to make.

Because she was still in mourning, the engagement took place quietly on St Valentine's Day the following month. As if to make belated efforts to atone for what had seemed his unfeeling behaviour after her bereavement, he told her several times that 'your father is watching us'.[12] Yet those closest to him found that he seemed extremely happy. His old tutor Hinzpeter noted that he allowed a glimpse 'of his feelings for Dona, quite unprecedented in their poetic and ebullient character'.[13]

'A brilliant 'parti' in the eyes of the world it certainly is not,' wrote the Crown Princess, referring to the betrothal, 'and that will wound the inordinate parvenu pride and vanity of the Berlin people who since 1871 think themselves the only great people in the world.'[14] After the engagement was officially announced by Emperor William at a family banquet in June 1880, she was annoyed that her eldest daughter Charlotte was pointedly cold-shouldering Augusta Victoria in public and encouraging others to do likewise. Several others at Court were also hostile to or at least distant with her, especially after it was rumoured that her grandmother was illegitimate and that such a marriage would somehow tarnish the name of the Hohenzollern dynasty.

The newly-betrothed prince wrote in measured if hardly enthusiastic terms in his diary that his marriage with the princess had been decided on, and was now official.

> I like the Princess. She is a charming, fresh, German girl, who will make a perfect Empress, and at the same time an excellent wife. My mother and father, as well as the Emperor and Prince Bismarck, are quite pleased at my having fallen in so readily with their views in regard to my betrothal, which in a certain sense is a political event, because it puts an end to a feud that has lasted something like fifteen years, and has reconciled our House with one of the minor dynasties that have had to suffer through the rise of Prussia.

He also noted that he had fulfilled an injunction given to him by Bismarck a year previously to marry another German princess and 'not to introduce another foreigner in our home'. As his future wife, she need not fear that he would ever be wanting in any respect and consideration towards her. He would know how to treat her and honour her, but he would certainly not allow her to have anything to do with his private affairs or those of the state.[15] They seemed very much the words of a future sovereign who was prepared to do his duty to the state, but hardly of the besotted husband-to-be whom his mother thought she had observed.

To his mother, William wrote 'most touching letters (in his own funny style) about his great happiness'. She had been aware that it would be an unpopular match at Berlin, as 'the poor Holsteins' were not sufficiently aristocratic, but comforted herself with the likelihood that 'this prejudice will wear off very quickly.' Fortunately she was able to tell Queen Victoria a month later that Dona had made an excellent impression on everybody at Berlin; 'Her smile and manners and expression must disarm even the bristly, thorny people of Berlin with their sharp tongues, their cutting sarcasms about everybody and everything. The announcement has been much better taken than I had dared to hope.'[16] The Grand Duchess of Baden was very impressed with her nephew's choice of bride, and found her 'wholly delightful, sweet, natural and uninhibited'.[17]

The young princess was undoubtedly bedazzled by the prospect of marriage to a future Emperor, but wise enough not to show it too openly. William and Augusta Victoria corresponded eagerly. In one letter she wrote how 'I, too, long for you so very very much, my heart's treasure,' and in another how much she was looking forward to the time when the wedding itself was over; 'I too cannot *express* how I am looking forward to the moment when after all the ceremonies we are *completely* alone with each other and I can flee into your arms after all the turmoil & excitement.'[18]

To his uncle Christian in England, William wrote in a rather stilted fashion that his fiancée had 'such a winning expression in her eyes, such a reassuring manner, and in addition her whole appearance makes such a noble and wonderful impression'.[19]

The Crown Princess proved to be a tireless champion of her new daughter-in-law at the Berlin Court. She knew too well from bitter experience that the lot of a bride of a future heir to the Prussian throne could be an unhappy one, and she did her best to give the young woman all the moral support she could. Perhaps she failed to appreciate that anything in the way of wholehearted endorsement from her, *'die Engländerin'*, whose presence was still strongly resented by Bismarck and others at Berlin, was not perhaps the best possible start the young bride-to-be could expect. At the same time, the Crown Princess had long had an increasingly difficult relationship with her eldest son, and she fervently hoped that her son's wife would be able to build a bridge between them once the marriage had taken place.

The sharp-tongued Empress Augusta, who had always been devoted to her grandson, also added some kindly words of advice. She warned the young woman that her husband would need 'much understanding love', and that it was 'the serious and difficult task of his wife to help him understand the true nature of his high office'.[20] Princess Augusta Victoria was joining the Hohenzollern family with the gift of a generous fund of goodwill.

- 2 -

Marriage, 1881-88

On 26 February 1881 Princess Augusta Victoria, the new bride-to-be, made her first entry into Berlin, as the procession in the city streets staged to welcome her, a brilliant imperial pageant, was watched by tens of thousands of eager spectators. It was temporarily interrupted by the intrusion of a float sponsored by the Singer Sewing Machine Company, no doubt aware of the potential publicity, featuring a seamstress busily plying her trade. Once noticed, the offending exhibit was speedily removed. The black and white Prussian flag with its black crowned eagle decorated the buildings along Unter den Linden as the procession started, with lines of military officers, troops and officials marching down the main thoroughfare in Berlin, and the city's master butchers in front, maintaining a time-honoured tradition. Next came the imperial carriage carrying the bride and the Crown Princess, covered with gold and glass, drawn by horses dressed in the Prussian military livery.

Augusta Victoria waved graciously to her future subjects, not letting herself be deterred by the fact that in accordance with Prussian court etiquette she was freezing on that bitter winter day in a dress which left her shoulders uncovered. Following the vehicle came the bridegroom on horseback, attired in the uniform of a captain of the imperial bodyguard. As they passed through the Brandenburg Gate, white doves were released from the top of the monument as a 72-gun salute was fired. The royal family then made their way to the Schloss where Emperor William, the Crown Prince, and a full military guard of honour were all waiting to welcome her as they entered the building to sign the final marriage contract between bride and groom. That evening celebrations took place throughout the streets of Berlin, with cheerful crowds parading the streets until late at night.

The wedding ceremony itself took place at the royal chapel on the following day. The bride wore a dress of gold and light blue fabric with diamonds adorning her head and neck, and a long train which had to be carried by six bridesmaids. Among royal guests present were three of the groom's uncles, the Prince of Wales and his brother Alfred, Duke of Edinburgh, Louis, Grand Duke of Hesse and the Rhine, his great-uncle Ernest, Duke of Saxe-Coburg Gotha, and King Albert and Queen Carola of Saxony. The six-hour Lutheran service, the Crown Princess wrote to her mother afterwards, was 'exhausting, suffocating and interminable as all the Berlin state weddings are,' and 'a harangue which the young couple listened to standing, and which is so cold and so funereal that one has not the impression of attending a wedding! Service it cannot be called.' Nevertheless she was full of praise for the young princess who in her opinion 'looked quite lovely, so sweet and self-possessed not shy and yet so modest and gentle. She wore a radiant smile on her face and her wedding dress became her so well. Even the stiff crown suited her.'[1]

As William took his wedding vows, he turned to face the Emperor with the traditional bow, as if asking him as head of the family for one last time for his permission to marry. At the request of the Crown Princess, a very large English wedding cake surrounded by orange blossoms was produced at the reception. The day's proceedings ended with the customary *Fackeltanz*, a torchlight dance usually performed at Prussian royal weddings and danced by the bride with all guests who held the rank of Royal Highness and above.

It was observed by some of the guests that the bridegroom seemed somewhat remote during the proceedings, and did not seem concerned about giving the impression of a blissfully happy new husband. His diary entry was short and to the point, his mind evidently focused more on his life as a soldier than on his wife: 'I was married to-day in the chapel of the Castle. We shall settle in Potsdam, where I am to continue my service in the Hussars of the Guards.'[2]

The wedding festivities lasted for several days. On the day after the ceremony Prince and Princess William made their first public appearance together as husband and wife during a carriage ride through the streets of Berlin. Along the route, crowds never ceased to clamour for a close glimpse of the couple. Augusta Victoria was unused to being the centre of attention and it was a new experience for her, but she played her part well, remaining radiant, smiling to everybody and showing genuine enthusiasm throughout. Later that week she and William received over two hundred royal deputations that had arrived in the city for their wedding. It was all a useful first taste of experience of her life in Prussia as the third lady of the land.

After the celebrations were over they settled in their official residence, the Marble Palace, Potsdam. Here they spent most of the first few years between their wedding and accession, their only other accommodation outside Potsdam being a few rooms at the palace in Berlin, fifteen miles away.

A little over two months later, on 10 May, the young couple were present at another important wedding, when they travelled to Vienna for the marriage ceremony of Crown Prince Rudolf of Austria-Hungary and Princess Stephanie of Belgium. William found Rudolf and his father, Emperor Francis Joseph, 'decidedly cordial' in their welcome, and was touched by 'the heart-winning friendliness and kindness' shown by Viennese court society to his wife.[3]

By the autumn the family were aware that Augusta Victoria was expecting her first child. A son was born at the Marble Palace on 6 May 1882, and a salute of 101 guns announced the glad tidings to the people of Berlin. History almost came close to repeating itself, for the mother's first confinement, like that of her mother-in-law had been before her, proved to be a difficult one. For a while mother and child were both in some danger. Outside the delivery room stood the Crown Prince and Princess, the Emperor and his aides, all in military uniform, as they anxiously waited for the father to come out and announce the birth of his eldest son and heir. The baby prince would be third in succession to the imperial throne.

The father was rather more expansive in his diary about the baby's birth than he had been about his wedding the previous year, although he seemed to be implying some mild criticism of his father:

> My son was born to-day. He is the first heir to the German Empire, and I feel that I have performed my duty towards this Empire, in providing our dynasty with a successor in the direct line. My grandfather is so happy, far happier than my father, at least outwardly. He never expected to have this wish of his granted before he died, to see his family continued by me. In the country, also, the event has been hailed with immense joy, and I have received any amount of congratulations.[4]

The baby was given the names Frederick William Victor Augustus Ernest, but soon became known as William like his father. Despite the difficult birth he soon flourished, and his mother made a quick recovery from her ordeal. To distinguish him from his father, the family called him 'Little Willy', a name which in view of his short stature would remain with him throughout life. The lack of height came from his father, who in addition to having a withered arm from birth was also slightly shorter than his wife. At table, particularly during official court functions, he sat on a cushion, as he did not like her to appear the taller.[5]

Now that she had provided the empire with an heir in the next generation, Augusta Victoria took on what some considered an air of haughtiness that had previously not been seen in her. When the Crown Princess brought her daughter-in-law some prettier clothes, telling her she owed it to William and herself to look more attractive, she said loftily that there was no point in getting her figure back as she was certain to lose it again soon as her husband intended to make the succession secure. The Crown Princess might have found this comment rather tactless, especially in view of the fact that only two of her four sons had survived to maturity. The third, Sigismund, had succumbed to meningitis at the age of twenty-one months, and Waldemar to diphtheria at eleven years, two losses that the grieving mother never really got over.

Augusta Victoria's mother-in-law was not the only member of the family to find her a less than ideal new member of the family. As children, William and his eldest sister Charlotte had always been close. Now married to Prince Bernhard of Saxe-Meiningen, she was an elegant, sophisticated young woman who did not care for her brother's slow-witted wife and made her views plain. Her parents had tried to persuade themselves that her bad behaviour to Augusta Victoria shortly after her engagement the previous year would only be a temporary aberration, but time was to show otherwise. Charlotte's husband Bernhard proved just as bad, and he bemoaned what he called her 'stupidity, lack of education, and tactlessness'.[6]

Any hopes that William's parents might have had that marriage would soften him and make him more amenable proved in vain. They would soon sadly discover than beneath Augusta Victoria's meek, submissive mask lay an influential, reactionary bigot whose small-minded views only served to reinforce his own. She hated the English, who in her eyes personified the worst excesses of liberal politics and immorality, and it was a hatred that would become more pronounced over the years. Whenever she needed advice from an older woman in the family she turned instead to her aunt Helena in England, and the one member of the family in England whom she liked and respected, or to her grandmother-in-law, Empress Augusta, or to Countess Waldersee, whose husband Alfred was a close associate of William and would later be his chief of the general staff. The princess and the countess remained close friends and had a common interest in religion, which they both took very seriously. It would later be said that 'for nine years they strove together to get all Germany down on both knees, one of them for God and the other for the Hohenzollerns'.[7] One of her particular *bêtes noire* was Leopold II, King of the Belgians, who was notorious for his immoral private life and cruel treatment of his relations. She further resented the fact that he attempted to persuade her husband, particularly after he became Emperor, to take part in certain business enterprises in Eastern Asia and Africa. To her it was imperative that he 'shouldn't listen to the plans of the horrible man'.[8]

Instead of acting as peacemaker, whenever there was a family argument she nearly always stood unreservedly by her husband. This in itself was not surprising, but she gave others the impression of not having a mind of her own and just following William's line for its own sake. She had also seen for herself or been warned that her mother-in-law, who had always been a little too fearless in speaking her mind with scant regard for the consequences since she was a young bride, had dearly paid for her independence of mind, and that in the interests of a quiet life she would be well advised to maintain the status quo.

But she was often concerned at the ill-feeling between William and his parents. In November 1883 there was a rather fraught occasion when the young couple came to visit the Crown Prince, apparently because they had to wait for a train to Potsdam after a dinner with Grand Duke Vladimir, younger brother of Tsar Alexander III. The Crown Prince accused his son of various discourtesies, and the latter replied with 'inane remarks about his time being filled'. After further short-tempered exchanges, William said he believed he was not welcome, especially since his father had been making it evident for some time that he 'could not stand' his son. The Crown Prince thought this was 'outrageous', he wrote to his wife, and demanded that he 'offer proof – which he could not do'. Feeling that the conversation was taking a rather ugly turn, Augusta Victoria said she did 'not want to leave with everyone in such a frame of mind', and the conversation continued, a little less unpleasantly at first. However they then began an argument about their differing political views, and the Crown Prince said that to his sorrow he could see that tension between father and son, 'which is traditional in the Pruss[ian] family has also set in with us'. Augusta Victoria implored him 'for God's sake not to say such a thing, or to let it happen, at which point the discussion grew calmer, and turned to parliamentary issues, the attitude of the parties, and the development of our constitutional life'.[9]

Yet too many bitter words had been exchanged between father and son. It was evident that there was a deep gulf between them which would not be easily bridged.

● ● ● ● ●

As personalities, husband and wife had little in common. The poorly educated Augusta Victoria was overawed by William's apparent cleverness, dilettantism, and restlessness. A God-fearing woman brought up to believe that her first duty in life was to make and keep her husband's home comfortable and give him sons, she was content enough not to ask for more.

Several of her contemporaries found her dull and lacking in personality. According to Daisy, Princess of Pless, clothes and children were the main subjects of Princess William's conversation and the only things that she thoroughly understood: 'For a woman in that position, I have never met anyone so devoid of any individual thought or agility of brain and understanding,' she noted. 'She is just like a good, quiet soft cow that has calves and eats grass slowly and then lies down and ruminates.'[10] William's cousin Princess Marie of Edinburgh, Crown Princess and later Queen of Roumania, an acute observer of her many relations, noted in her memoirs that Augusta Victoria was a good mother and wife, 'but her amiability had something condescending about it which never rose to the height of cordiality or ease; there was effort in it. Somehow her smile seemed glued on; it was an official smile.'[11] Stephanie, Crown Princess of Austria, with whom she was initially on good terms and also came to write her recollections some years later, considered that she did not get on very well with her, 'for I found it hard to discover what she was really interested in'.[12] In the diary of Emily Loch, lady-in-waiting to Princess Christian of Schleswig-Holstein, there is a reference in the early 1880s to having 'ordered paints for Pss William'.[13] This suggests that she evidently continued to dabble in her childhood interest of art during her spare time, though there seems to be little if any reference elsewhere as to what extent.

When Queen Victoria welcomed Prince Henry of Battenberg as her youngest daughter Beatrice's future husband in January 1885, Augusta Victoria was ready to join in with the general criticism from her husband and his grandparents of Henry's morganatic birth that he was not of sufficiently royal blood. The Queen was furious when she heard of their attitude, especially as her granddaughter-in-law was in no position to criticise. She wrote to the Crown Princess castigating 'the extraordinary impertinence and insolence and, I must add, great unkindness of Willie and that foolish Dona'. Particular scorn was reserved for the latter, whom she called a 'poor little insignificant Princess, raised entirely by your kindness to the position she is in'.[14]

At this there was a whiff of hypocrisy in the air, for Augusta Victoria herself was of hardly more noble birth than the Battenbergs. As the Queen and her eldest daughter had warmly endorsed her despite the fact that she was not as pure-blooded as some of those at the Prussian Court would have liked, it was a clear example of double standards which did her no credit. Yet in all fairness, Augusta Victoria could hardly have dared to take issue with her husband on such an issue. The Crown Prince and Princess did not attend the wedding of Beatrice that July, but the young couple paid them a visit at Potsdam on their honeymoon, during which William and Augusta Victoria ostentatiously made a point of snubbing them.

It was fortunate for William that his wife was such a submissive young woman, almost as if she was overawed in having married the man who would become the mightiest Emperor in Europe. She soon found that being his wife was no bed of roses, and that there were sacrifices to be made. It shocked her to discover that he kept a loaded pistol in his drawer all the time, and that he was a hypochondriac who constantly fussed about his health. His friends and courtiers thought he made it obvious, to the point of rudeness, that his clinging, cloying wife bored him if not incurred his resentment, and that he found her excessive domesticity stifling. He made no secret of the fact that he sometimes found married life a chore, and that during their early years at least he looked on her as little more than a brood mare.

His constant love-hate relationship with England came to the fore when he bemoaned her simple, rather provincial upbringing, away from a genuine royal court, saying publicly that it was easy to tell his wife had not been brought up at Windsor but rather in Primkenau. The Crown Princess might possibly have a little pleased at his admission of British superiority, something he did all too often, but this was surely outweighed by her disgust at his sheer tactlessness. Augusta Victoria strongly resented this rude remark about her childhood home, and it may have only served to reinforce her hatred and resentment of everything British. In later years her Anglophobia became ever more pronounced.

William was not always the most faithful of husbands. Unlike his 'uncle Bertie', the Prince of Wales, he managed to keep his affairs with various mistresses out of the public eye. Nevertheless he had a few anxious moments when they threatened to tell the world as he proved remarkably tight-fisted when it came to paying them off for services rendered, and only the readiness of Bismarck to intervene and make arrangements for payment of the necessary sums prevented scandal. It was rumoured that one young lady became pregnant in 1882 and presented him with a daughter in secret, though this remains unproven. One must assume that Augusta Victoria was aware of the gossip at least. Yet if so, she must have accepted the guiding principle of many another royal and imperial wife of the age who knew that her duty was to accept, if somewhat reluctantly, that there was one rule for men and another for women.

While they rarely threatened to cause any scandal, Augusta Victoria's own family could be something of an embarrassment to her, particularly in her last years. Her mother became increasingly eccentric with age, in what was probably an early and as yet unrecognised manifestation of obsessive compulsive disorder, perhaps exacerbated by early dementia. She had developed an obsession with washing, and divided her body into several areas, each of which she insisted required different utensils and linen. It was also said that she made 'unspeakable assaults upon her male neighbours at table'.[15]

Encephalitis and depression, with violent mood swings, hallucinations, and severe headaches were also part of the picture. At the same time the widowed Duchess had a worrying tendency to attack people physically for no apparent reason, especially at the dinner table. Any efforts by her daughter and ladies-in-waiting to calm her down were counter-productive, resulting in her losing her temper, swearing aggressively, and breaking glasses. At length William, angered by their futile efforts to keep her under control, declared that she could only come and stay three times a year and no more, and only one, two or three weeks – or as long as the household could put up with her.

Augusta Victoria's sisters were easier to get along with, although Louise Sophie was a lively young woman with a disturbingly independent streak. Her brother Duke Ernst, generally known as Ernst Gunther, proved amenable at first, but was regarded as something of 'a clinger', one of those relatives who when invited was impervious to hints in due course that he might have outstayed his welcome. Within a few years he, too, would become well known for his laddish behaviour which was hardly commensurate with the dignity of his august sister and brother-in-law. The worst instance of this would manifest itself when he and his mistress were implicated in the 'anonymous letters' scandal from 1891 onwards, with accounts of parties including senior aristocrats, court officials and members of German royalties and much sexual misbehaviour. Although nothing was proved, it was believed that the writer primarily responsible was Ernst's mistress, who was henceforth banished from the borders of Germany as a result.

William's relations with his family were not exactly harmonious either. He adored and revered his grandfather and grandmother, but with his parents it was a different story. While he had more in common with them than he cared to admit, he thought his father was far too much under the influence of his mother, a misconception which had been deliberately fostered by Bismarck and others at Court who had a vested interest in creating disharmony between them. He got on well enough with his only surviving brother Henry, but while he and his eldest sister Charlotte had previously been close, the latter's contempt for her sister-in-law gradually altered the situation.

With his other three sisters, whom he contemptuously dubbed 'the English colony', he had very little in common. His passionate love-hate relationship with Queen Victoria wavered between two extremes. On occasion he was sometimes heard to wish that she was dead, but as a rule he generally looked up to and had great respect for her, and he was always keen to be invited to stay with her in England.

The Crown Princess had always been fond of Augusta Victoria. She not only hoped that the love of a good woman and wife would soften her eldest son's increasingly hard and cruel character, but also trusted that she would take kindly to a little gentle reassuring help and guidance to prepare her for life at Court, and would come to look on her as a good friend and mother. Sadly, on all three counts, the Crown Princess was to be disappointed, and all her well-intentioned offers of help were to be rebuffed, not always kindly. Augusta Victoria had been made well aware by others, her husband above all, that with her English sympathies the Crown

Princess would not be a worthy or popular mentor, and she pointedly kept her distance from her mother-in-law. In addition she was not particularly bright, and could never by any stretch of the imagination be considered an intellectual. Such qualities, or lack of them, made her a perfect wife for the egocentric, demanding Prince William of Prussia. At the same time they made her a decidedly uncongenial daughter-in-law.

When Queen Victoria learnt from her daughter that Dona was proving hard work and asked her why she had championed her so hard, the Crown Princess replied with sadness that in her opinion she had always seemed likely to make an excellent wife and mother. She and Fritz had always been very fond of her father, and particularly liked the girls as children. 'I then hoped and thought she might be grateful and affectionate to me,' she added, but was forced to admit that 'in that my hopes have been completely disappointed.'[16]

Although she could hardly have expected otherwise, Augusta Victoria soon learned that being wife of the prince who was second in succession to the throne would mean that husband and wife would have very little time to themselves. From the beginning of their married life, she would see him at breakfast, before he left to go to his military duties as Commander of the First Regiment of the Foot Guards, to which he had been promoted by Emperor William shortly before his wedding. These revolved around manoeuvres, parades and similar activities. He generally returned to the palace for lunch, and if he had no further military commitments in the afternoon, he sometimes took her for a ride into the countryside around Potsdam, but they were never alone as he always took his aide-de-camp with them.

His wife was probably not surprised to learn that the army and all things military were his life, and that he saw his soldiers more often than he saw her. From the age of twenty, he very rarely wore anything but military uniform. The Prussian court was nothing if not militaristic from top to toe. It was very much a man's world, and Princess Daisy of Pless spoke for many when she said that Prince William 'thought little of us women; he almost despised us.'[17] He was particularly good at arranging to be away from his wife on manoeuvres or hunting whenever she was expecting, and her letters to him were full of desperate pleas for him not to stay away for too long, as she found the separations 'awful'. After he went chamois hunting in Switzerland in the autumn of 1881, she wrote to tell him how brave she had been after his departure, until the evening; 'on going to bed I was no longer able to hold back my tears'.[18] If she had ever hoped for an attentive, thoroughly domesticated husband, she was to be rapidly disillusioned.

True to her word, Augusta Victoria did indeed make the succession safe, for William, later to become Crown Prince, was followed by Eitel Frederick in 1883, Adalbert in 1884, and after an interval by Augustus William in 1887. Two more sons and a daughter would follow in the next reign and make the family complete. She was devoted to her children, and loved playing with them in the nursery. From an early age, the princes were inevitably inculcated with the traditional Prussian love of all things military. They were given toy lead soldiers and little cannons which discharged peas to play with. 'Little Willy' was encouraged in his war games, in constructing strongholds of sand, fortresses of pounded earth, and even digging up flowerbeds and grass plots outside the palace windows.

● ● ● ● ●

Though his health was generally robust, in September 1886 William was struck down with a very painful ear infection shortly after he returned from a visit to Russia. His physician informed Augusta Victoria that the illness was quite insignificant, but a few days later the infection spread and his condition became serious. He underwent emergency surgery, and at one stage she feared for his life as she sat by his bedside, holding his hand and praying. By the end of October he was pronounced out of danger, and as he recovered, husband and wife had found a new closeness.

Not long after this, Augusta Victoria's father-in-law became unwell. During the autumn of 1886 Crown Prince Frederick William had a severe cold that he could not shake off. Some months later, in March 1887, at a speech he gave at the dinner given to celebrate the ninetieth birthday of his father the Emperor, it was noticed that his previously resonant voice seemed less powerful than before. In the spring he consulted throat specialists who called in a Scottish laryngologist, Dr Morell Mackenzie, who had a practice in London. For several months, he and the German doctors argued about their imperial patient, whom they feared was suffering from cancer.

When he knew that his father was unwell, William took it for granted that he and Augusta Victoria would be representing the Hohenzollerns at Queen Victoria's jubilee celebrations in London, marking her fiftieth year on the throne, in June 1887. Mackenzie told the Crown Prince and Princess that he would recommend them to come to London for the summer, which would not only enable them to take part in the festivities – something which they certainly did not intend to miss – but also to allow the Crown Prince to be examined and treated at his consulting rooms in the English capital while he was there.

Devoted as she was to her husband, Augusta Victoria shared the view of most of the family, and indeed of Bismarck himself, that he was still too young and not yet ready for the arduous task of Emperor. She confided her views to Count Waldersee, who noted in his diary that it was becoming ever clearer that he could be called on at any time to succeed to the throne. 'The Princess Wilhelm,' he wrote, 'is a thoroughly sincere and upright woman and she clearly spoke her mind when she said that she wished the Kaiser a long life with all her heart and that she feared Pce. Wilhelm was still too young for the position of Kaiser.'[19]

After the jubilee festivities were over, the Crown Prince and Princess went to stay at Balmoral. Dr Mackenzie recommended that his patient should avoid the bitter inhospitable weather of Berlin during the winter, and early that autumn they went to the warmer climate of San Remo on the Riviera. They had only been there a few days when unfavourable symptoms appeared, and after a further examination in November 1887 the doctor had to admit that the growth on the Crown Prince's vocal cord was carcinomatous. It was tantamount to a death sentence.

In February 1888 he underwent a tracheotomy in order to facilitate his breathing, but by this time he had virtually no voice left, and it was evident that he would not survive for long. During the previous few months the nonagenarian Emperor William had had several strokes and was becoming ever more feeble. The German empire thus had the sorry sight of a sovereign and his heir who were both dying, and it was not impossible that the latter would predecease the former.

When Emperor William passed away on 9 March 1888, less than a fortnight short of what would have been his ninety-first birthday, a telegram was sent to his son and daughter-in-law, now Emperor and Empress, at San Remo. Although they were aware that the sudden move from the hospitable Mediterranean climate to a bitterly cold and snowy Berlin would be anything but beneficial for him in his poor state of health, the gravely ill monarch and his consort made immediate preparations for the return by train to their capital. It was impossible for them to evade their duty and there was no alternative but for them to go back. The new Crown Prince and Princess were waiting for them on the platform station at Charlottenburg, with everyone deeply moved as the towering but now painfully gaunt figure of Emperor Frederick III stepped down from the train and embraced his son and daughter-in-law. Now voiceless, he had to write down everything he wished to say on a pad of paper.

If William and Augusta Victoria, now expecting another child, were moved by the plight of his parents, they did nothing to show it. Everyone knew that it would only be a few weeks if not days before they would be Emperor and Empress themselves. As the Empress Victoria wrote bitterly to Queen Victoria exactly one week after their accession, 'I think people in general consider us a mere passing shadow, soon to be replaced in reality by the shape of William.'[20]

As she was expecting another child, the new Crown Princess spent much of her time resting, as she waited for her husband to succeed to his inheritance. At the beginning of June the Emperor, Empress and their three younger unmarried daughters Victoria, Sophie and Margaret, moved from Berlin to their summer home, the Neue Palais at Potsdam. Shortly after they had settled there, the Emperor gradually lost ground. William, Augusta Victoria and the rest of the family were warned that the end was approaching, and they were all standing around his bed on the morning of 15 June as he passed away.

- 3 -

The first years as Empress, 1888-96

At the age of twenty-nine, William was German Emperor, with Augusta Victoria by his side as Empress. On his orders a guard had already been placed around the exterior in order to prevent anything or anyone from leaving the premises without his full approval, and he lost no time in ordering his soldiers to ransack the palace in search of any correspondence of documents that might incriminate his parents, or suggest that his mother had been a British agent. As a despairing Queen Victoria wrote to Princess Louis of Battenberg early the following month, 'It is too dreadful for us all to think of Willy & Bismarck & Dona – being the supreme head of all now! Two so unfit & one so wicked.'[1]

Augusta Victoria was fortunate in having a perfect excuse for keeping her distance from this unpleasantness. At the time she became Empress, she was almost eight months into her fifth pregnancy. On 27 July she gave birth to another son, who was named Oscar.

If the Empress Frederick ever had any hopes that Augusta Victoria might understand her misery and help to build bridges between her and the Emperor, these would soon be dashed. It was all the more galling for her as she had done more than anybody else to bring them together and help to make the marriage possible. According to one rather gossipy biography, based on the letters of Augusta Victoria's lady-in-waiting Ursula, Countess von Eppinghoven, during the hours after Emperor Frederick's death and as the Emperor and his men were seizing control of the palace which was now his, the Empress Frederick begged her daughter-in-law to stop desecrating her home, and speak to him with the authority of a wife and mother. Unless she expected to be treated by her sons as she herself had been treated by her son during the previous two hours, she implored her, 'restrain him, re-establish me as mistress within my own walls, and I will be for ever grateful to you.' Moved by her mother-in-law's plight, the new Empress went into the library but returned after a few moments, her face flushed and trembling as she said she could do nothing. William was there in his capacity as Emperor, and she could not interfere with his official business.[2] But the episode is uncorroborated elsewhere, and may or may not have been a product of the Countess's imagination in part at least.

Whatever her private feelings may have been towards her mother-in-law, within a year or so the new young Empress had become quite insufferable. She displayed an air of arrogance which grated on her mother-in-law and sisters-in-law. 'She has <u>quite</u> forgotten, or does not like to remember, or really does not understand what she owes me,' the Empress Frederick lamented in a letter to Queen Victoria in March 1890. 'She has a great sense of duty, but she does not seem to see <u>what</u> her duty towards <u>me</u> is!'[3] Moreover she was full of pride, 'and she thinks she knows better than everyone because she is the Empress.' She meddled in everything that anybody in the family did, every small trifling matter was reported to her, and she gave orders in a way that everybody else found very galling.

A few months later, she was acknowledging that her daughter-in-law was trying to be pleasant, but with limited success, as she 'means to be very kind to me, but she has something condescending & patronising which irritates me, & rubs me up the wrong way; - & she orders her sisters in law about as if she were the Empress Augusta, which makes me <u>frantic</u> sometimes.'[4]

The young Empress's Anglophobia also created a rift between herself and the Emperor on one hand, and Prince and Princess Henry on the other. Since his marriage in May 1888 to his cousin Irene of Hesse, who had always got on extremely well with her family in England and had been a good influence on her relatively unassuming husband, Henry had found himself less at ease with his brother and xenophobic sister-in-law. Irene, who appropriately in view of her name soon acquired a reputation as the family peacemaker, reported to Queen Victoria that her aunt Vicky would be much happier if only she would 'try & look more kindly on people's motives', and that she felt the same about Dona, 'who I know deeply sympathises for poor Aunt Mama [the Empress Frederick] & has often told me that she was so terribly unhappy how often she was misunderstood by her whenever she tried to do anything to please her & that she tries her best.'[5]

In view of 'Dona's' habit of ordering Irene and the rest of the family about at the behest of the Emperor, one cannot but wonder if Princess Henry, a comparative newcomer at the Berlin court who had to watch her position with care, was being a little too charitable towards the new Empress at this stage. As other letters would show, she got on extremely well with her aunt and mother-in-law, who would be eternally grateful to her for her efforts to bring the family together. Other relations who visited the imperial court at Berlin similarly found the Empress's manner off-putting, disliking her heavy-handed sense of moral and social superiority.

●●●●●

Though Augusta Victoria had never had any significant contact with Crown Prince Rudolf of Austria-Hungary, both she and the Emperor were deeply affected by his tragic death by suicide after killing his mistress Marie Vetsera at his hunting lodge at Mayerling, when they learned of the news on 30 January 1889. The horrified Emperor, who had met him several times but had little sympathy for his comparatively liberal politics, found it difficult to believe that he had taken his own life, while the Empress broke down in tears.

Neither of them attended the funeral at Vienna, but after a memorial service held in Berlin they lingered for some time afterwards at the Austrian embassy so they could demonstrate their deep sympathy and heartfelt distress. When the Emperor was preparing to pay a first visit to Rudolf's grave in September 1890, she wrote to say how grateful she was that the course of his life had been so different from that of 'a friend of your youth in the same position in life...One can easily see there what a difference it makes whether someone has built on the right ground or not!!'[6]

A further bone of contention had arisen within the family at the beginning of 1890. Dowager Empress Augusta, widow of Emperor William I, and nominal head of the German Red Cross, had died in January at the age of seventy-eight. As the Empress Frederick had had plenty of experience in organising and founding charities, as well as nursing during the Franco-Prussian war of 1870-1, she would have been the obvious choice as her daughter-in-law's successor, and she expected that the position would be offered to her. Only after the aged Empress's funeral did the Emperor curtly inform his mother that he had already asked his wife to take on the position. It was a disappointment that rankled deeply.

In November 1890 the Empress was about eight months pregnant with her sixth child. When they were attending the wedding of William's second sister Victoria to Prince Adolf of Schaumburg-Lippe, his third sister Sophie, who had become Crown Princess of Greece thirteen months previously on her marriage to

Crown Prince Constantine, chose the occasion to announce her intention of entering the Greek Orthodox Church. She had intended to inform the Emperor, as head of the family, but before she had a chance to do so, she received a command from the Empress to come and see her at once. The heavily pregnant Empress told her that as head of the Lutheran Church, the Emperor would never permit her to change her religion. If she disobeyed him and did so, then she would 'end up in hell'. Taking the perfectly understandable point of view that her loyalty was to her husband and new country rather than her brother, Sophie politely but coldly told her sister-in-law that it did 'not concern anyone here' and she did not need to ask anyone. Her brother William, she said, had 'absolutely no religion'; if he had, then he would never have behaved to their parents as he did. Whether she went to hell or not was her own affair, and it was not for the Empress to concern herself about it. The latter reportedly grew purple in the face with rage, and became so excited that the doctors had to be called in to see her.

Next day the Emperor angrily called on his mother with an ultimatum to the effect that, if Sophie entered the Greek Church without his permission, which he certainly would not grant, he would forbid her to set foot in Germany again as long as she lived. He telegraphed to King George of Greece that should she persist in doing so, 'I shall no longer regard her as a member of my family and will never again receive her. I beg you, as far as in your power, to dissuade her from her intention.'[7] The King replied with great restraint that he did not feel justified in trying to influence his daughter-in-law. Though he was too tactful to do so, he would have been entitled to point out that she was not only a married woman but also a Greek subject, and thus no longer under the jurisdiction of her elder brother. King George, the Empress Frederick wrote to Sophie, 'has the best of the argument, and I admire him for being so gentle and moderate, in spite of such provocation.'[8] When the Empress Frederick declared that she was equally supportive of her daughter's intentions, and agreed that it was none of his business, the Emperor complained that she had nothing but scorn and contempt for Christian belief. She told him that if he carried out his threat to ban Sophie from Prussia, in future she would no longer visit or receive him. Afterwards he told one of his officials that his mother had treated him so badly that he was reduced to tears.

Sophie had never been close to her brother, and she was not at all worried by his outbursts or by the attitude of her sister-in-law. The Empress Frederick found Augusta Victoria's attitude exasperating; 'Poor thing she seems to think that she has to exercise a sort of police supervision of the whole family in <u>all</u> things! This is not called for either by her position or her age or her experience. The Empress Augusta whose ideas were of another century also thought this, & Dona fancies she has stepped into <u>her</u> shoes (over my head) and must continue this! To me it is most galling!'[9] Nevertheless she suggested to Sophie that she might like to extend an olive branch to her brother by writing him a conciliatory letter explaining fully her reasons for wishing to adopt the Greek faith. When he still would not give way, she sent her mother an open telegram saying: 'Received answer, keeps to what he said in Berlin, fixes it to three years. Mad. Never mind. Sophie.'[10]

The Empress became ill, gave birth three weeks prematurely on 17 December to another son, Joachim, and according to the Emperor 'for two days was at death's door'. He still nursed a grievance against his sister, on the grounds that she had been responsible by causing his wife to become unduly excited, and against his mother for apparently encouraging her. When the Empress Frederick came to call upon her daughter-in-law in order to enquire after her health and that of the new baby, he would not allow her to enter the castle, but immediately gave orders that she was to be taken back to her carriage and sent away.

The prematurely born Joachim did not turn out to be healthy. He was far weaker than his brothers, and suffered from epileptic fits from infancy. The Emperor evidently blamed his poor state of health on his sister, and the argument continued for several months. As late as May 1891 he was complaining almost hysterically to Queen Victoria on the subject. Sophie, he wrote, had caused 'an awful scene in which she behaved in a simply incredible manner like a naughty child which has been caught doing wrong.' He then had an interview with Sophie, in the presence of the Empress Frederick and Crown Prince Constantine, in which his errant sister entirely refused to acknowledge him as the head of her family or church, declared that she would not have anything more to do with the Hohenzollern family, or with their country, and refused to answer any questions he asked her about her ideas about changing or not, declaring that it was nobody's business. If 'my poor Baby dies,' he concluded on a note of hysteria, 'it is solely Sophy's fault and she has murdered it.'[11]

Yet the Emperor's threat to banish his sister did not materialise. Queen Victoria wisely predicted that nothing would happen as long as Sophie continued to visit Germany as usual, provided that Constantine was with her. When the family travelled to Heidelberg to call on the Empress Frederick later that year, the Crown Prince of Greece arrived a few days before his wife in order to see what reaction if any there would be from his brother-in-law. As he had suspected, there was none at all. The Emperor was due to make a state visit to Britain, and he did not wish to incur the wrath of his formidable grandmother, so Sophie was informed and she duly followed her husband into Germany.

The Emperor's forthcoming visit to England was certainly not being looked forward to by those who would have the dubious pleasure of entertaining him. Marie Adeane (later Marie Mallet), a lady-in-waiting at court who was noted for her sometimes sharp-tongued comments on some of the royal guests with whom she came into contact, had not yet had the dubious pleasure of meeting him. But she noted in her diary in the spring of 1891 that everybody around her was dreading his arrival, fearing what he would say and do once he was there, and not speaking any more kindly of his wife. 'The more I hear of him the more I dislike him, he must be such a despot and so terribly vain,' she wrote. 'However, poor man, he has a most insipid and boring wife whom he does not care for and from whom he escapes by prancing to the four corners of the world'.[12]

Courtiers were quick to realise that the Empress 'bored and agitated' her husband. She doted on him with cloying admiration, and her efforts to calm his mercurial temper or to keep his fragile ego intact sometimes only seemed to have the opposite effect in that they contributed to his nervous and restless character. In June 1890, when he had decided to spend a few days at Wilhelmshaven after a Scandinavian cruise, instead of coming straight back to Berlin to be with her again before leaving for England, again without her, she wrote to him that it made her cry to think that if only he had come back she could have been with him for almost three days, and that it was very hard 'when one loves one's little husband so much'. She could not wait to welcome him home again; 'God grant that our days together in Berlin will be all the nicer, as the children are all away and we can pretend that it is our first married year.'[13] Those who observed the couple at close quarters were convinced that, during the early years at least, she fussed after him to a degree which he probably found suffocating, and from which he found it vital to escape from time to time.

Always very religiously-minded as a young woman, 'the insipid and boring wife' became increasingly dogmatic with age. The composition of her personal household did not help matters.

Her ladies-in-waiting were Evangelical Lutherans, all from high-ranking aristocratic families with unblemished reputations, chosen carefully for their positions for their unimpeachable moral characters above all else. These prudish if not downright bigoted females became her closest friends, though some of them were not above mimicking her behind her back. Three of them in particular, Countesses Mathilde Keller, Claire von Gersdorff, and the senior, her Mistress of the Robes, Therese von Brockdorff, who never left her side, were known derisively by her husband's entourage as the 'Hallelujah aunts' for their obsessive devotion to Protestantism. Her cousin by marriage Princess Alice of Albany, who would have been about seventeen at the time she saw them, found them 'formidable females' and suspected that the Empress was rather afraid of them, particularly as she always seemed to accept their decisions without question.[14] The Empress's critics accused them of being as conservative, agrarian and strictly evangelical as she herself was, and the Emperor sometimes found their excessive piety as wearisome as everyone else. Between them, the Empress and her ladies encouraged church attendance every Sunday and insisted on it among members of her household.

Small-minded and xenophobic as well as piously orthodox, she was passionately anti-Catholic, even to the point of having Roman Catholics excluded from her retinue or among her personal servants. On a visit to Rome in April 1893, she almost caused a major international incident when at first she refused to pay a courtesy call on Pope Leo XIII, convinced that as the leading Protestant lady in Europe she should have nothing to do with him. It took a good deal of persuasion from her husband to induce her to change her mind, which she did with very bad grace. While he was no partisan of Catholics himself, he found the passionate Protestantism and religious bigotry of his wife and her ladies bordering on the excessive.

Some of those who knew her readily took a more sympathetic view. Some years later, according to her daughter-in-law Cecilie, the Crown Princess, her whole existence was filled a with a deep and genuine sense of piety, and 'she clung with her whole soul to the Evangelical faith from which she received so much strength and courage.'[15] The children's governess, Ethel Howard, also claimed that she was not the religious bigot of popular legend, insisting that she was merely 'a great advocate of Protestantism', and that while she was criticised for 'adhering to its tenets in a narrow and unenlightened manner, to my mind she seemed to look on other creeds and forms of Christianity with a broad and kindly tolerance.'[16]

● ● ● ● ●

Nevertheless, for all their faults, the Empress and her ladies spent much time in working alongside their mistress for charities, and their piety helped to shield the court from scandal. Throughout her husband's reign she was liked and respected for her charitable works. Motivated by her upbringing, she was always active in promoting charitable causes, took a keen interest in the welfare of the poor and the sick, and received many petitions on a daily basis from people or organisations requesting her help. It was said that she read every letter addressed to her, even begging letters, made enquiries as to how deserving the writers or causes she was asked to support might be, and answered as much of her correspondence as she could by hand herself. When the sheer volume made this impossible, she dictated replies to her secretaries, who were not permitted to answer any communications without consulting her first.

One of the first organisations with which she had become involved after her marriage was the Elizabeth Children's Hospital in Berlin, of which she became matron, and where she made a point of visiting the patients on a regular basis. An active advocate of building and restoring churches in and around Berlin, she attended rallies put on by the Reichstag's right-wing Christian Democratic Party. She was also actively involved with the Berlin City Mission, and in 1888 she founded the Aid Society of the Evangelical Church, which became the Protestant Women's Mission in 1897. The advocacy for young women was a cause always especially dear to her heart, and she also showed forward thinking when she founded the Elberfield House of Refuge, set up to help neglected infants and young children at risk. In this, she was following a worthy example set in England by her aunt Helena, who had long been active in helping to set up and administer charitable organisations in Windsor and London for those unable to help themselves. Passionate about the education of women, she was credited by some as having done more than anybody else in Germany to make public careers open to women as well as men, encouraging them to work for their own living.

Within a few years she was sparing no effort in taking on public work in the charitable sector, confined to the traditionally female areas of childcare, education and health. Hospitals were a particular concern of hers, and she devoted much time to visiting wards, particularly those of children, her motivation for doing so the positive side of that strict religious faith for which she was sometimes heavily criticised.

The German people who were aware of her efforts on behalf of such causes were devoted to her for such kindness and obvious sincerity. While she did not have the organisational flair or ability of others, it did not deter her from taking over concerns which had been initiated by the two previous German Empresses. She therefore supported them as best she could, perfecting in her public as in her private life the role which suited her best, that of mother. As her own children grew up, they never lost their great attachment to her, or the sense that she would always be their best friend. She might be over-protective towards them, but they all adored her for it.

● ● ● ● ●

It was unfortunate that the Empress, so keen to do good for her people, did not have the gift of getting on well with her own family, or rather that of her husband. Another personal problem came about when the independent-minded Princess Adolf of Schaumburg-Lippe, the second of the Emperor's sisters, incurred the wrath of Countess Brockdorff, at a function taking place at court on his birthday at which all those present had to offer him their congratulations. She was standing with her back to the window, and as there was a particularly cold east wind on that January day she slipped a sable boa over her shoulders to keep warm. Suddenly she felt a sharp tap on her back and a sharp whisper of 'Take that boa off.' Turning round angrily, she found herself face to face with the Countess, who told her that she could not possibly wear such a garment as her sister-in-law the Empress was not wearing one. The princess glared at her, retorted in a whisper (as talking was not permitted during the ceremonies) that the boa would remain on, and moreover that she would speak to her brother about it afterwards. She kept her word, and that was the last she ever heard of any such orders.[17] While the Empress could not necessarily be blamed for such minor upsets, the inflexible attitude with which she presided over court functions was at least partly responsible.

Yet the sister-in-law who gave the most trouble was the frequently mischievous and often less than respectful Charlotte, Princess of Saxe-Meiningen. A story was told that in November 1892 the royal stables at Berlin were preparing for the annual St Hubertus hunt early in the morning. Among those who arrived to take part were Charlotte and her lady-in-waiting, Baroness Ramin. The Emperor's sister had reportedly 'indulged in a lively breakfast', and loudly announced to them all that she would demonstrate how her sweet sister-in-law mounted a horse. When the animal was ready for her, she ascended the platform and let herself fall into the saddle with a thud that caused the animal to stagger. 'Just like a majestic sack of flour, is it not?' she cried as she rode off. Word soon got back to Her Majesty, and within hours everyone was informed that ladies, including Princesses of the blood royal, were not wanted at the forthcoming outing.[18]

As in so many other imperial and royal courts, etiquette was followed without the slightest deviation. At all formal functions involving a meal, dishes were invariably set in front of the Emperor and Empress first. The moment they had finished, everybody else at table had to give up their plates, even those who had been served last and had barely had time for even a mouthful. The children who were seated furthest away always went hungry, and had to take what opportunity they could to speak secretly to the servants below stairs in order to receive a small portion of leftovers. If there were no special receptions or other events, during the evening the Empress stayed at home in the palace while the Emperor went to a military review or meeting. Elderly generals found such occasions a penance, as they had to stand in his presence for several hours, never being invited to sit down.

Her piety did not prevent her from displaying what some at court considered an excessive love of luxury and pleasure. Family festivities became ever more grandiose and expensive, and it was considered by some that she wore an extravagant quantity of jewellery, and not always with the greatest sense of style. The Emperor was partly to blame, as he only encouraged her in her love of finery. In December 1893 his friend Philipp, Prince Eulenburg, at that time German ambassador to the court at Vienna, described her appearance to his mother at a concert at the Neue Palais when she had appeared 'in a gown of blue velvet combined with yellow muslin, large diamond and sapphire jewellery – not very well dressed.'[19]

● ● ● ● ●

After she had given birth to six sons, in September 1892 the Empress had a daughter, who was named Victoria Louise. Now that he had plenty of male heirs, the Emperor was not averse to being father of a daughter as well, and in adult life she was the only one of his children with whom he would ever really enjoy a harmonious relationship. He treated his sons like small recruits to be kept under strict discipline, and when they were old enough, he ordered them to follow him on long early morning rides on horseback. Fearing that this was putting too much of a strain on them, she begged her husband to let her accompany him instead. Though she was always exhausted by the time they arrived back, she took their sons out for a gentler ride afterwards so that William could not complain that they were poor horsemen from lack of practice.

With her lack of interests elsewhere, apart from the church, it was not surprising that she should immerse herself deeply in her children and family life. Her husband allegedly once remarked that she was to be 'nothing but a broodhen'.[20] Though she must have been hurt by such a patronising attitude which he presumably never bothered to conceal, she suffered in silence. Her children were a never-ending source of affection to her, and she became a keen photographer of them when they were small, keeping their baby teeth to be set into rings, preserving their hair clippings and giving them out as gifts. She supervised their early education, and as they were growing up, she clung on to them as long as she could.

The Crown Prince paid a glowing tribute to his mother in his memoirs:

> All that was best in our childhood, nay, all the best that home and family can give, we owe to her. And what she was to us in our early youth, that she has remained throughout our adolescence and our manhood. The kindest and best woman is she for whom living means helping, succouring and spending herself in the interests of others; and such a woman is our mother.[21]

As she knew the Empress Frederick adored children, Augusta Victoria kept her family at arm's length from her mother-in-law. At Joachim's christening she had refused to let the older woman hold him, saying coldly that the Emperor did not wish it as she was not the godmother. It was as if she regarded her mother-in-law as so Anglophile that she did not wish her children to become contaminated or develop anything in the manner of English ways from her. On the rare occasions when her children were allowed to visit their grandmother at her home, Friedrichshof, they did not generally feel welcome. From an early age, young Victoria Louise was aware of the family tensions. Her Greek and Hessian cousins, the children of her aunts Sophie, Crown Princess of Greece and Margaret, later Landgravine of Hesse-Cassel, were apparently indulged and allowed to do what they liked in front of their grandmother, while she and her elder brothers were not. Any noise from them would be met with a scolding, such as the admonition that they were 'not in a zoological garden!'[22]

Other members of the family also found there was a hard side to the Empress. Her younger sister Louise Sophie had also come to live in Berlin as the wife of Prince Frederick Leopold, a second cousin of the Emperor, whom she had married in June 1889. A more lively, outgoing and opinionated version of her sister, she was unable to forget the wrongs that she and her family had suffered at the hands of Bismarck and the late Emperor William I. She intended to go on being very much her own person, and when she clashed with the court's rules she inevitably found herself clashing with her sister.

The worst argument came on one cold winter day in the first week of January 1896. Prussian princesses, particularly married ones, were not allowed to take part in active sports, on the grounds that such activities were unladylike and undignified for the first family in the land and those most closely connected with them. Despite this edict Louise Sophie went skating at her home, Glenicke Castle, Potsdam, as she did regularly during the winter, with one of her ladies, Baroness Colmer. However this time they were unfortunate enough to break the ice, fell through, and for a while they were both in danger of drowning in the freezing waters below. Such foolhardy behaviour was bad enough in the eyes of the Emperor and Empress, but they compounded it by committing an even greater offence in their eyes by trying to cover up their tracks and conceal what they had done.

Although at most other Courts, such a misdemeanour would have been considered too trivial for anything more than a reprimand, but this would not be the case at Berlin. Prince Frederick Leopold was summoned before the Emperor, and upbraided for letting his wife behave in such a careless manner. When the Prince argued fiercely with the Emperor and told him bluntly it was none of his business, he was told that they would be placed under house arrest under armed guard. Then it came to imperial ears that the princess had committed another sin, by receiving a bicycle for Christmas. When the Empress heard of this, she wrote stiffly to her sister that neither the Emperor nor she would ever approve of a Prussian princess riding a bicycle, either in their own garden or anywhere else.[23]

Augusta Victoria was noted at Court for her freezing hauteur, and for being a stickler when it came to enforcing regulations according to the letter of the law. Ethel Howard was once spoken to firmly for sneezing in her presence, and told it must never happen again. Sneezes were considered a potential danger in the household for the Emperor was susceptible to chronic, even dangerous bouts of ear infection, and had a horror akin to mania of anything that might pass on cold germs. Miss Howard also discovered to her cost that the Empress once turned against her on the word of an old family nurse, and for a while she would not even speak to her in person. Any lady, princess or housemaid could expect to be admonished, even in public, if any small item of her dress or attire did not fully meet with imperial approval. Louise Sophie regularly found her inflexibility very irritating, and considered that by degrees 'the iron of Prussian discipline entered into her mental habits, if not into her soul.'[24]

The Empress's sense of moral propriety made her very much a Victorian, and she did not forgive those who transgressed the strict code of etiquette that enveloped the Hohenzollern court. Divorced people were anathema to her; women who had left their husbands were forbidden from the imperial court, and she actively intervened to prevent their former husbands from retaining positions in the government. When Count Paul von Hatzfeldt, German ambassador to London, divorced and took a second wife in 1895, she refused an audience with the latter. On being asked to intercede, the Emperor refrained from overruling her, on the grounds that such matters were the domain of the Empress, and that he could not order her to receive somebody who had made herself unacceptable to society. It was significant that the Emperor would never interfere in anything his wife did concerning household and its management at the Palais, and he accepted all her arrangements without question.

Court entertainments were traditionally the preserve of the Empress, but she was no lover of society life. In her formative years, she had never learned how to entertain or throw fashionable parties. Moreover, her husband's regular travels abroad meant that foreign visitors were rarely seen in Berlin. Dignitaries did not often come to court either, as many of them cordially disliked the Emperor, and were thoroughly vetted by the Empress. Her sense of propriety excluded her from holding audiences with men unless her husband was there as well. At a dinner she once refused to be seated next to Jules Herbette, the French foreign minister, because she considered his conversation vulgar. Even remotely suggestive anecdotes and jokes incurred her wrath, and at a sign from her, the royal party would leave plays, ballets and opera if there was the slightest hint of offensive dialogue or indecent dress. Herbert Bismarck, who had served as foreign minister while his father was in power, was another *bête noire* of hers, not because of his over-indulgence in alcohol so much as his love of telling of improper jokes and stories, even in the presence of ladies. In addition to her strict views on royalty not riding bicycles on the grounds that it was indecorous, she also maintained that men should keep their coats on when playing tennis.

Court life in Wilhelmine Germany was undoubtedly dull, and the Empress was regarded as an incorrigible prude. As the mother of six sons she tried to ensure that none of them were exposed to the temptations of 'fast' women, such as the American socialites whom her husband liked to invite to court and who lacked moral compass. However boys would be boys, and particularly in the case of her eldest son this proved a failure.

According to Prince Bernhard von Bülow, a future imperial chancellor, the Empress was German through and through, and she disliked foreigners. 'She thought Russians were barbarous and light-minded, Frenchmen immoral, and the Mediterranean races untrustworthy; the British, in her eyes, were a race of selfish and unscrupulous hypocrites, for whom she felt even less affection than the rest.' He thought that she 'displayed a stiffness and reserve towards foreigners' that did nothing to improve German relations with such countries as Russia, Britain and Italy in particular. While her husband was inclined to overdo his affability towards foreigners, 'she often went to the other extreme.'[25]

Between the British heir and his wife Alexandra and the German Empress, there was never any love lost. His lifestyle, his love of gambling and mistresses, greatly offended her sense of propriety, while she was aware that the Princess of Wales resented her and her family for their positions as rivals for the duchies of Schleswig and Holstein, even though they might have found a common cause in that the fathers of both of them had suffered at the hands of Bismarck.

The Princess of Wales also despised the way in which the Empress had totally taken her husband's side against her mother-in-law. As a good and loyal wife she could have hardly done anything else, but the British heir's wife considered that as a woman the least she might have done was to attempt to build bridges between them. One of the very rare occasions on which the Prussian-hating Princess of Wales had been persuaded to cross the North Sea and set foot in Germany was when she joined her husband in attending the funeral of Emperor Frederick in June 1888, as a gesture of solidarity with the persecuted widowed Empress Frederick. Throughout her nephew's reign she would be one of the least frequent of royal visitors to his empire.

Outside her circle of ladies, the Empress had few friends at court or indeed among the family. Her father had died when she was only twenty-one and her mother, with her severe mental issues which worsened with age, was no support either. Like her mother-in-law before her, she had been left to fight her own way. In the case of the latter, who did at least have the advantage of a devoted and always supportive husband, there had been much prejudice against the intelligent, strong-minded young daughter of Queen Victoria. In the case of Empress Augusta Victoria, she was a distant cousin not considered sufficiently high-born, and not very clever. Though lack of cleverness was regarded as more of a virtue in Hohenzollern circles, sometimes it could be a case of being unable to do anything right. People never forgot her modest background, and even her husband, who could be notoriously cruel to other people when it pleased him, did not stop short of making dismissive remarks against her family origins. It was particularly regrettable that she had not shown more kindness to the Emperor's mother, who would almost certainly have been a valuable ally even though she knew that her word carried little weight at court or with her eldest son. The only other relation from that generation, the sharp-tongued Louise, Grand Duchess of Baden, her aunt by marriage, was always ready to overwhelm her with instructions about what to do and what not to do, while demanding complete obedience in the process on the grounds that she was twenty years older and therefore more experienced.

It was fortunate for her husband and his family that in spite of the way in which she controlled certain aspects of court life, Augusta Victoria was by nature one of those meek, compliant women who at other times was prepared to obey and do what was asked of her. With her origins which were a little more humble than those of her in-laws, perhaps a part of her never ceased to be dazzled by her good fortune in having married the man who was without doubt the most powerful sovereign on mainland Europe, and she felt she owed it to the family as well as herself to make the marriage work. Part of her duty was to absorb the system and enforce it as strictly as those around her always did. Crown Princess Ferdinand of Roumania noted that while some people were ready to ridicule her, she always 'admired the patient courage with which this devoted woman carried out her husband's every order; there was a brave abnegation about it which is not given to every woman.' She did not think that the Empress 'enjoyed all the racket and fatigue, but the characteristic smile never faded from her lips'.[26]

Nevertheless, during the years ahead the Empress would assume a more dominant role in supporting an increasingly weak-willed husband than anybody, not least the husband himself, would ever have imagined at the start of their marriage – and at no little cost to her personal health. While she did not profess to have the same political mind as her mother-in-law, this did not preclude her from giving good advice where she felt the occasion demanded. In July 1896 she wrote to the chancellor, Prince Chlodwig of Hohenlohe-Schillingsfürst, that if he was willing to help the Emperor along, she had faith that everything would turn out all right for them. While she was anxious not to be seen to be 'meddling in politics', if she thought that ministers were making matters difficult for her husband, she always felt obliged to help and try to smooth things out.

> I have always wanted the Emperor to have older more experienced friends who would help here and there with a calm word or good advice. For despite his exceptional gifts – I as his wife say this with pride, there probably is at present no other monarch in Europe as gifted as he – he is still young, and in his youth one is apt to act spontaneously.[27]

The general sentiments in this letter might almost equally have come from the pen of his mother or his grandmother in one of their most conciliatory moods.

Certainly during the early years of her husband's reign, she was careful to maintain absolute discretion. She spoke about politics only with her immediate entourage, and even then she was always reserved and cautious.

Sometimes people would catch a glimpse of the more likeable woman beneath the hard exterior. The Empress Frederick, a kindhearted woman who was always ready to see the best in others despite the way she had been treated at the Berlin court for so many years, wrote to her daughter Sophie after a visit in the autumn of

1891 that Dona had been 'very grand and stiff and cold and condescending at first, but became much nicer afterwards. Perhaps it was also partly shyness.'[28] Her errant sister Louise Sophie, with whom she got on well, also conceded that when she was 'not bowing to the will of her autocratic husband she was easy and indulgent'.[29] Her cousin Alice of Albany, who was sometimes mildly critical of her older relations, found her 'most affable and kind'.[30] Moreover she was unfailingly gentle and sympathetic towards small children, with whom she always felt at ease. On one public occasion a little girl had been briefed to present her with a bouquet, but when her big moment came she was so frightened that she was sick over the Empress's hand. Unruffled, the latter was the first to kneel and comfort the child.

- 4 -

The end of the century, 1897-1901

In August 1897 the Emperor and Empress paid a state visit to Russia. On the majority of his trips abroad the Emperor had gone without her, but this time she accompanied him on what was her first expedition to St Petersburg. William got along satisfactorily with Tsar Nicholas II, but the same could not be said of their wives. The women plainly had little in common, and the Tsar was unimpressed by the Empress. He commented to his mother, the Dowager Tsarina, after they had left, that she 'did her best to be pleasant but looked awful in sumptuous gowns completely lacking in taste; in particular the hats she wore in the evening were frightful.'[1]

Criticism of the Empress's dress sense also came from other quarters. Another contemporary, probably Countess von Eppinghoven, remarked that her everyday habit, a black costume and silk hat, was 'not at all becoming'. In uniform, the same observer declared, she looked 'a perfect fright', not merely because of the dress so much as because of her cocked chapeau, replacing the cuirassiers' steel cap. This was made of white felt, brim pinned thrice up, the crown bent in and trimmed with white ostrich-tips, with an *aigrette* or crest of brilliants. The combination, she wrote, was 'entirely unsuitable to the imperial lady', especially as the Empress's weak eyesight made it necessary for her to add a tulle veil to protect her eyes from the sun.[2]

By this time she had been suffering from a nervous condition for some years, which suddenly became worse. Over the years she had taken care to keep herself fit, walking, playing tennis and riding during the summer. Time after time she dutifully accompanied her husband as often as she could on his trips abroad, often to places and to other people whom she thoroughly disliked. In addition to giving birth to seven children, by the age of fifty she had had at least one or two miscarriages.

A particularly stressful period led to a complete breakdown towards the end of 1897. Augustus Eulenburg, senior master of ceremonies at the court, informed his cousin Philipp that she was suffering from 'severe nervous shock' and for a while nobody could get any sense out of her. The Emperor suggested that a short stay on the Riviera would do her good, 'an idea which did not please the All-Highest patient at all, and now we are engaged in the cross-fire which we have seen so often'.[3] She stayed in Berlin, while the press made regular allusions to her 'having been indisposed for some time', or having to cancel engagements because of a cold, and after a period of convalescence in Homburg in March and April she made a slow partial recovery during the early weeks of 1898.

By summer she seemed to be restored to good health. Among her husband's ministers, few played a more supportive role than his secretary of state for foreign affairs, Bernhard von Bülow, and on 16 June she wrote him a letter of deep gratitude:

> Seeing that man and wife belong together, I cannot but send you a word of thanks on this tenth anniversary of the Kaiser's accession, for your aid has saved him from many an annoyance and has, thank God, enabled him to carry out many plans for the good of the country. I send you this portrait as a sign that I, too, mean to try to do my share of work for the Kaiser, even if it is at times no more than to soothe him in his days of worry, when he is often overwhelmed with plans and decisions. How often in quieter past days did I use to consult with your poor brother, Adolf, for the sake of the Prince, as he then was; he, too, I was always sure, only considered everything in so far as it would be best for the Kaiser.[4]

Yet all was still not well, as the Emperor confided to Eulenburg during a Scandinavian cruise in July 1898. The latter passed on the Emperor's comments to Bülow, telling him that 'the poor woman's nerves' had been ruined by child care and royal duties, and that His Majesty feared her present calm state could not possibly last. There had recently been 'a fight', or more probably an argument between husband and wife which resulted in a tantrum on her part during which she came closing to lose all control of herself. It was followed by angry scenes between Countess Brockdorff and the Emperor, which culminated in the latter ordering the former out of his presence. In addition, he complained angrily about the 'intolerable disturbances' which his wife inflicted on him while he was working or resting, 'by constantly bursting in and pestering him with nursery matters'.[5] In his opinion, peace was prevailing for the time being, but he felt that it was only a matter of time before such issues and problems recurred.

Despite his wife's fragile temperament, only a few days later, after their return from the cruise, the Emperor saw fit to admonish her firmly with regard to her obligations to the state. His relations with Bismarck had been stormy since the latter had resigned the chancellorship in March 1890. Yet when the latter died on 30 July 1898, aged eighty-three, the Emperor was anxious to be seen to treat him with all due respect. The Empress had never been able to forgive him for what he had done to her family's status, or what she regarded as his 'dethronement' of her father. At the time she was about to travel to Coburg to attend the wedding of her brother Ernst Gunther to Princess Dorothea of Saxe-Coburg. When she asked him to propose a toast to her brother and his bride-to-be two days later, he firmly refused. Just before he was due to travel to Friedrichsruh for Bismarck's funeral, he ordered her to dress in mourning immediately and treated her to a long lecture in front of several senior ministers and others. He emphasised that the German people would never forgive her if she showed any lack of admiration for the recently deceased chancellor.[6] She obeyed, but with a great show of reluctance.

At least she had the consolation of knowing that her brother had chosen a good and thoroughly German bride. Some six years earlier, in the autumn of 1891, he had made a tentative offer of marriage to Princess Victoria Mary of Teck. Notwithstanding her German origins, she had become one of the most English of princesses and would never have given serious consideration to a marital future in Germany. Within two years Mary, always known in the family as 'May', was married to George, Duke of York, second in succession to the British throne after his father, the Prince of Wales. When the Empress was told what a charming girl May was, according to her mother-in-law, the Empress was much offended, and told her that her brother 'would not dream of making such a mésalliance!!!'[7]

While the Emperor always had a rather complicated love-hate relationship with England, she became more and more Anglophobe as time went on. In the spring of 1899 she wrote to Bülow, begging him to intervene. The Emperor has told her that he had been invited by Queen Victoria to Cowes in August.

This seems to me quite beyond belief! Perhaps he cannot be prevented from going to see his grandmother, but I do beg you to prevent him from sailing again at Cowes, especially on board the Meteor. He could quite well go in the Hohenzollern, pay a visit to the Queen, and then come back. After all that has happened, to mix again in that society, to expose himself to the risks of this sailing, and, last not least, time after time, to let himself be beaten at the last moment by some trick of the English, this makes me too furious, both for the Emperor's sake and my husband's. I hope you will prevent it.[8]

Bülow knew better than to try and prevent his Emperor from doing what he wanted in the way of social visits, and the Cowes-loving imperial sailor went regardless. Not for the first time his sporting efforts were rewarded when he won another cup.

● ● ● ● ●

In the second week of November 1899, Tsar Nicholas and Empress Alexandra came to Potsdam, paying the German sovereigns a short visit while they were travelling back to St Petersburg from Darmstadt. Diplomatically it achieved nothing, and it was overshadowed by the poor health of Alexandra. Moreover, any goodwill that might have been created by a personal meeting between the sovereigns and their consorts was immediately banished by a tactless action of Empress Augusta Victoria at the end. Etiquette required her to accompany Alexandra to the station at Charlottenburg before her departure but she did not, giving as a rather unconvincing excuse the fact that she was wearing a décolletée dress. In fact, her real reason was that as a good Protestant – as she liked to think of herself – she had never forgiven her Russian cousin for her change of religion, and did not like her English ways.[9] It was an act of pettiness which rankled deeply with and was never forgotten by the departing Russian sovereigns.

Many of William's visits abroad were without his wife, but a few days after the departure of Nicholas and Alexandra, he paid a visit to England and insisted that she join him. She had sided wholeheartedly with the Boers against the British during the Boer War, being at one with her ladies, the Reichstag and the majority of the German people in disapproving of the visit at a time when British 'mammonism' was trying to strangle 'the brave and godly Boers'. She told Bülow that she heartily hoped the visit would be

49

cancelled, as it was quite impossible for them to be seen going to England at such a time. While she had taken his advice and been careful not to say anything to the Emperor about it, she was sure that 'very soon now our ships will be burned. I am afraid it will do the Kaiser any amount of harm in the country if we really go. Britain is only out to make use of us. Of course, it is frightfully difficult for the Kaiser, but at bottom I think he would be glad to get out of it.'[10] After a period of indecision she agreed to accompany him to Britain with two of their sons, Augustus William and Oscar, but she made no attempt to conceal her reluctance.

They arrived at Portsmouth on 20 November and travelled by train to Windsor. While they were there a state banquet was held at St George's Hall in the castle. To her extreme displeasure she was seated next to the Prince of Wales, a relation whom she despised because of his lack of morals and free and easy approach to mistresses. As her own husband had not been above taking the occasional mistress himself, this mounting of a metaphorical high horse suggests a degree of double standards.

In 1900 two family deaths affected the Empress badly. On 25 January her mother Adelaide died at Dresden after an attack of pleurisy, exacerbated by heart trouble. Nine months later her cousin Christian Victor of Schleswig-Holstein, a promising young man who had always been liked and respected by all his relations, died of enteric fever while serving with the army in South Africa. Although her sympathies had always been strongly with the Boers, her uncle Christian and aunt Helena and their children had been almost unique among the British royal family with whom she got on really well. The loss of both coincided at a time when her health had been giving cause for concern, and indeed that of the Emperor as well.

After a North Sea cruise that summer, Count von Eulenburg reported with alarm that His Majesty had such a violent attack of rage that he himself was quite frightened, fearing the Emperor was 'no longer in control of himself', while his doctor feared a weakening of the nervous system. In September his bad temper gave way to paranoia, he complained about a 'suffocating web of senseless court ceremonial', and said that he was 'constantly surrounded by a network of spying lackeys of the Empress'.[11]

Since William disliked plump women, Augusta Victoria subjected herself to medicines and strict dieting in order to keep her figure. Her physical appearance was under constant scrutiny from her husband. He ensured that she had a regular supply of diet pills to keep her figure trim, and as a result her slim figure was said to be legendary in royal and imperial circles. Moreover, he was so insistent that she should look the epitome of feminine elegance that he maintained strict control of her wardrobe, and even designed many of her dresses himself which he insisted she must wear with her opulent rows of sparkling jewels, diamonds, wide hats which he selected. As her hats and dresses sometimes came in for savage criticism behind her back, it can be assumed that his sense of fashion and eye for haute couture did not accord with that of everybody else.

In addition to seven pregnancies, she had had at least two miscarriages which she tried to keep from her husband. Her health suffered accordingly and General Adolf von Deines, who was in charge of the young princes' education, lamented having 'to deal with a nervously ill woman and an unreasonably anxious mother, who, despite many excellent qualities, hurts at least as much as she helps – strictly from anxiety.'[12] Sometimes the meek and adoring consort tried the Emperor's patience so much that he wanted to send her away, persuading her that it would be for the good of her own health, but she always resisted. If he did not want her to be too fat, the opposite could be true as well, as he sometimes taunted her with being too thin.

For once this moved her to protest, and she begged him to stop criticising her as it only saddened her. She complained that it was only natural for her nerves to be 'not the best & in particular will suffer even more if I have to be separated from you so often. Of course it is impossible under such circumstances to become fat. So please stop rebuking me for it, it only makes me sad….As regards food, I am stuffing myself with all sorts of nourishing things; I can't do more than that.'[13]

At length everything came to a head. For some time she had been increasingly intolerant, short-tempered and inclined to snap at those around her. William was alarmed lest his wife might have a long-dormant hereditary disorder which would mean she might need to be admitted to a sanatorium. Her hair suddenly turned white, and her face looked blotched, puffy and aged. She flew into rages over trivial matters, reproached William for preferring the company of Eulenburg to hers, and made terrible scenes when he refused to take her on his trips around Germany. They had long argued regularly about their sons' upbringing. In 1896 he had planned to send the two eldest, the Crown Prince and Eitel Frederick, to the Plön cadet academy, and though she begged him not to, he remained obdurate. Now, four years later, he decided that Princes Augustus William and Oscar should go there too. She insisted that they stay in Berlin with

51

her, wept through the night, and bitterly accused her husband of not loving her and trying to escape her company.

During a hunting trip to their hunting lodge at Rominten in September 1900 there were several scenes between husband and wife. After one violent argument she ran after him, as Eulenburg reported to Bülow, 'like a hunted deer (I won't say like a hunted cow)', in the presence of other people. He was surprised that she did not have a stroke there and then, but she was evidently 'in a bad nervous state'.[14] The Emperor told Eulenburg that he was almost at his wits' end as to how to cope. He complained that the Empress 'made scenes' all night long with her weeping and screaming, and he could not stand it any more. She was making herself ill because she could not be a 'middle class' mother, a devoted wife, and a reigning Empress all at the same time. He feared that if matters became worse, she might end up being confined in a 'cold water treatment hospital'.[15]

Eulenburg did his best to reassure him that she was suffering from temporary nervous disease of some kind, and that the only problem was to find a proper medical cure. The first step would be to separate her from her sons, Oscar and Augustus William, but that she should keep the youngest, Joachim, and her daughter with her, and all three should go and spend a long time somewhere in the country where it was quiet with good air. He, the Emperor, could then go and see her at intervals, but if his sojourn was to last longer than a fortnight, leave after the first scene she made with him. The danger of losing him would have to bring her to her senses. Again he told her that his word was law, and the boys were sent to the academy at Plon.

After a few days the situation had evidently not improved, and Eulenburg advised him that in view of her strange behaviour it would be better for them both if he was to sleep in a separate bedroom and locked the door. Some of the family suspected that his main concern was less her well-being, more the embarrassment of having a wife who behaved in such a manner and whose mental health was possibly open to question. At one stage she reportedly accused him of having an unnatural relationship with Eulenburg, whose homosexuality was being furtively whispered about by only a select few who were aware of it. Eulenburg was a helpful father figure who for some years had provided him with moral support, advice and friendship, something he had not been able to obtain elsewhere, and at her lowest ebb she resented the fact that he seemed to find his company so much more congenial than hers. Eulenburg himself was well aware that she was jealous of him, and she disliked her husband having long visits from his friends, so it would be very unfortunate if she was to hear about their conversations.

Fortunately, by winter 1900 she was recovering. Though she was by nature neurotic and remained liable to clinical depression at times, she seemed to have learned how to deal with her mood swings and behave more normally. When her husband had similar problems about eight years later, partly as a reaction to what would prove the most severe crisis of his reign before the war, she would manage to draw on inner strengths to a degree that few people around her would ever have anticipated.

Her recovery came just in time, for within the next few months two more bereavements, not totally unexpected, would strike at the heart of the family. For the last two years the Emperor's mother, who had lived more or less in retirement at her newly-built home Friedrichshof, near Kronberg, had been increasingly unwell. After a fall from her horse in September 1898 she did not recover as quickly as she expected to, and medical examinations shortly afterwards confirmed a diagnosis of cancer. By autumn 1900 she was too ill to travel overseas, although she was longing to make one final visit to the land of her birth again, and she was confined to her home at Friedrichshof. At one stage in October it was believed that she was about to die, although she rallied slightly.

No sooner was she out of immediate danger than it became evident to the family that for her mother the end could not be far off. Queen Victoria, who had celebrated her eighty-first birthday in May, was in increasingly poor health. The deaths in July 1900 of her second son Alfred, Duke of Saxe-Coburg Gotha for the last seven years, and of one of her favourite grandsons, Christian Victor of Schleswig-Holstein three months later, and continual bad news from South Africa during the Boer War, had upset and saddened her, and soon after Christmas 1900 it was apparent that she would not last much longer.

In January 1901, Prussia was celebrating the bicentenary of the Hohenzollern monarchy. One of the highlights was a march past, in freezing cold weather, as the soldiers marched in procession past the Schloss and saluted the Emperor and Empress. Among the guests invited to the festivities at Berlin was Arthur, Duke of Connaught who, apart from the Prince of Wales, was now Queen Victoria's only surviving son. A particularly military-minded prince, he was one of the British royal family with whom the Emperor had always enjoyed cordial relations. After the Emperor had made a speech, he was informed that the Duke had received a telegram from England, informing him that his immediate return was advised as Queen Victoria was seriously ill. The Emperor promptly cancelled the remaining celebrations and travelled with the Duke of Connaught to Osborne, joining the rest of the family as his 'unparalleled grandma', lay in her bed slowly sinking. Meanwhile the Empress went to Kronberg to be with the desperately ill Empress Frederick, who she knew would be devastated by the news which everybody knew was only a matter of time. According to Empress Augusta Victoria, even her mother-in-law did not think he ought to stay in England and wait for the funeral, as she was very anxious to see him again herself. 'The great lady is in a terrible state,' she wrote to Bülow. 'Her spirit is wonderful. I do not think her condition will be worse as a result of her mother's death, she had already calmed down sufficiently.'[16]

Irritated at and possibly jealous of the emotional bond which he had always had with his 'unparallelled grandmama', the Empress strongly disapproved of his being in England at all at such a time. Queen Victoria died on the evening of 22 January with her family around her bedside, the Emperor helping to support her during her last moments with his good right arm. The Empress asked Bülow to do what he could to dissuade him from staying for the funeral at Windsor Castle on 2 February, insisting that he could perfectly well allow his brother Prince Henry or the Crown Prince to represent him. As an extra excuse, she reiterated that his mother was dangerously ill and she particularly wanted to see him again. She [the Empress Frederick] was very anxious to go to England herself, but in her condition that was impossible, and this made her 'restless and miserable'.

It was to no avail, for this was one family occasion which the Emperor was determined he would never miss. The new sovereign King Edward VII made him an English Field-Marshal, and this gesture also incurred her wrath. 'If this is not an irony in present circumstances, I do not know what is,' she declared angrily. It is supposed to be a gracious act, but I consider it tactless. The Kaiser, of course, has got to look pleased.'[17] Britain was particularly unpopular in Europe, especially in Germany, because of the Boer War. Although King Edward was undoubtedly motivated by family considerations and ties of blood, he surely appreciated that to offer his nephew a controversial honour which he could hardly refuse would probably have caused him some discomfort at home, not least with his Anglophobe wife. The Emperor was being feted by the English at a time when he was at his most emotionally vulnerable.

The Emperor returned to Germany in February. It was not a moment too soon for the Empress, who like the senior ministers feared that the longer he stayed, the more like his English-loving sisters he would become. Once he was back, for a while the ruler who was constantly changing during the day from one military uniform into another was now hardly ever to be seen wearing anything but the civilian clothes which he had sported in England, including a tiepin bearing his grandmother's initials. The officers who were sent from Frankfurt to dine with him were astonished to find him thus attired, and even more to hear his constant enthusiastic allusions to England and everything English, which ranked far above German habits and customs.

Next he had to prepare for a visit by King Edward, who was coming for what he knew would surely be the last time he would ever see his favourite sister again. The Empress Frederick was now bedridden, apart from on warmer days when she would be taken out in her wheelchair and gently pushed around the gardens at Friedrichshof.

By the end of July it was clear that her sufferings would soon be over, and the rest of the family were warned that she was not expected to last for more than a few days. For the last few weeks her three youngest daughters, Victoria, Sophie and Margaret, had been taking it in turns to help nurse her, never far from her bedside. The Emperor and Empress joined them on 3 August and were by her bedside two days later when she passed away.

With her death, a force which had for a while been something of a rival to Empress Augusta Victoria was now gone.

Once again, within minutes of her death the Emperor sent his officers to ransack desks throughout the house in order to seize any private letters still stored there which he did not wish kept for posterity. As had been the case before Emperor Frederick's death, she had been aware what would happen. Her correspondence from Queen Victoria, much of which did not paint her eldest grandson in a very favourable light, had been taken to England several months earlier by the Empress's godson, King Edward VII's private secretary, Sir Frederick Ponsonby.

Although the Empress Frederick had been pushed into the background by the official world at Berlin during her widowhood, she had still been able to undertake a large amount of work on behalf of some of her charities. With her death, Empress Augusta Victoria was no longer living in her shadow, and felt she could expand her influence into different areas without fear of criticism or comparison to her mother-in-law who had, despite her son's best (or worst) efforts, still been much loved in Germany.

Ironically, it was at around this time that the Empress, now aged forty-two, was expecting another child. Her daughter, the youngest, was aged eight, and everyone had assumed that she was destined to remain the last. Perhaps aware that at her time of life it was unlikely that she would carry this last infant to full term, the Empress went to great efforts to hide her condition from her husband. She defied the orders of her doctors to rest properly as she accompanied him to his manoeuvres and then to Rominten. In September she paid the price and accordingly suffered a miscarriage.

Rather unsympathetically, Eulenburg remarked to Bülow that her love for her husband was 'like the passion of a cook for her sweetheart who shows signs of cooling off'. He also noted that 'this method of forcing oneself upon him is certainly not the way to keep the beloved's affection'.[18]

- 5 -

The new century, 1901-08

In October 1901 Empress Augusta Victoria celebrated her forty-third birthday. Now in middle age, her famed regal bearing remained undimmed, and she still looked every inch a sovereign. Her head and neck were often adorned with some of imperial Germany's most precious ornaments. The two previous Empresses had rarely made much use of the crown jewels, but Emperor William was lavish in the gifts he showered upon his wife, who relished wearing the finest of gemstones and diamonds.

After the difficult time she had been through at the turn of the century she had recovered to some extent, though she had become very stout, and within a few years her health would give increasing cause for concern. She gradually became her husband's rock, and her moments of frantic anxiety had become few and far between, replaced by a quiet submissiveness and determination to add strength, prestige and stability to the house of Hohenzollern. For the Emperor, a man who was driven by emotion and sentiment, her influence started having a calming effect on him. One contemporary observed that she 'acquired a considerable influence over her husband precisely by the way in which she effaced herself and subordinated all her thoughts and actions to his'. She made a point of never offering advice to him, but instead waited for him to come to her, and he therefore learned to look up increasingly to his wife with various problems.[1] The role which she played was in a sense comparable to that in the eighteenth century of Queen Caroline of England to King George II, a monarch who for all his good qualities was less wise and intelligent than his consort.

Her support of him covered other issues as well as emotional ones. Marriage to the Emperor had made her realise how fragile his ego was, and in her efforts to be a true helpmate, she did all that she could to try and become part of his life. She took pains to memorise the uniforms of his various regiments, forcing herself to read books on military subjects that she knew interested him, and accompanying him on his daily horseback rides. When he went out hunting, he tried to make his wife so uncomfortable that she would not want to come again, ensuring that she came along through all the dirt, mud, and rain, but she would not be put off. She also joined him on his early morning calls on his officials, and when he would allow her to, on his expeditions abroad.

Like him, she was very much a creature of habit and believed in following a daily routine. She awoke each morning at 6.00 and joined him for breakfast in their dining room, an area to which servants were never admitted. This was the one hour in the day which the Emperor devoted completely to domesticity, when they could gossip and discuss matters alone and in secret. After breakfast, she reviewed the daily kitchen menus and consulted with each member of the household on plans for the day. She then went to see her children before they began their lessons. Much of the rest of the day was spent working at her desk. Her daughter Victoria Louise would always remember how busy her mother was. Her earliest childhood recollection of her evoked a picture of her constantly writing; 'I can still hear the continuous scratch of her pen on her diary as I went into her sitting-room.'[2]

Her children deeply loved and respected her. When it came to the upbringing of the youngsters, she made it clear that their mother needed to be in charge. She once told his childhood friend Poultney Bigelow that though her husband was German Emperor, she was Empress of the nursery. No matter how busy or tired she might be in the evening, she always made it a priority to check up on her children in the nursery before she went to bed. One evening the princes were eager to receive a goodnight kiss from her, but she was attending a function with the Emperor and they were not expected back until very late. The princes assured their mother that they would stay awake until she returned, and they did so – until well after midnight. When she asked them how they had managed to stay up so late, little Willy explained that he and his brothers had tied a string to each other, and when one started falling asleep, the others would tug on the string to wake him up. Later he wrote in his memoirs, in moving terms, that in their formative years she was always at the centre of their existence.

Throughout their life together she was and always remained her sons' confidante, adviser and intercessor. If they wanted to speak to their father, they were required to secure permission first from their tutor or military governor, but they could always approach their mother any time they wished. Their father was an unfailingly strict disciplinarian who rarely indulged his sons, particularly the eldest three. In due course this would lead to strained relationships between the sons and their father.

When any of them misbehaved, it was always their mother who would cheerfully go and smooth matters over with her husband. This was particularly the case with the Crown Prince, with whom the father often had minor differences. 'Little Willy' was inclined to rebel against the strictness of his upbringing, in the same way that the Emperor as an adolescent had often challenged his parents' views. He also publicly aligned himself with the political far right parties in the Reichstag, who tended to criticise the Emperor for being insufficiently nationalist and aggressive. As if that was not enough, he showed signs of modelling himself as a personality on his great-uncle King Edward VII, whom he admired and who had in his younger days been notorious for his affairs. This, needless to say, came as very bad news to the Empress.

In spite of this, part of the boys' love for their mother was rooted in her strong moral character. When they were young, they had regular lessons on teachings from the Bible. One day the teacher said, 'There is no one without sin.' Eitel Frederick immediately insisted that this could not be true, for his mother had never sinned. They all shared her love of outdoor activities, and she was particularly fond of tennis, which she played with all the family – no doubt with the boys keeping their jackets on. Because of her love for the sport, the Emperor had had tennis courts installed at all the family's residences. Her favourite activity was riding, and she tried to do so every day if time permitted. Such activities were not without their minor hazards, for she had occasional accidents and falls from her animals, as well as a fall from vertigo while playing tennis one day.

Nevertheless, as her young boys became young men and began to think for themselves, they did not always accept their mother's rigid etiquette at court. The atmosphere was so staid that the most recent and fashionable American dances such as polkas and two-steps were forbidden, being regarded as not really respectable or dignified, and even drinking (except in great moderation) and smoking were not really approved of. On one occasion when a ball was given in honour of the visiting Prince and Princess of Wales, the musicians in the band were ordered by the Emperor not to play any modern songs, as he maintained that court balls were not held for personal pleasure but for lessons in personal diplomacy. Two of the German princes, probably William and Eitel Frederick, had an argument with the band on the subject, but as the latter were obliged to obey only the Emperor, his sons' intervention was to no avail.

As the unfailingly honest, never-sycophantic Countess von Eppinghoven had noted, the Empress 'was endowed with virtues more sturdy than nimble, and dancing is entirely out of her line'. In her younger days she would dance once or twice a year at private balls held at the imperial apartments in Berlin. A few days before one such ball in the winter of 1893, she said that she planned to trip the light fantastic at the request of His Majesty. Before doing so, she asked the Countess to ensure that the musicians would be well hidden by the plants, for she did not wish them to see her dancing. If necessary, perhaps a screen could be strategically placed to render her invisible. When the lady said that a screen might spoil the airy decorative effect, the Empress pointed out that then the Emperor would be displeased. A reminder that her husband's great-grandmother Queen Louise was passionately fond of dancing and enjoyed doing so in public proved to be of no avail, as the Empress insisted that she could not 'bear the idea of gyrating round under the vulgar eyes of hired attendants and servants',[3] and it would be beneath her dignity.

By middle age the Empress's health was not at all good. She was prone to spells of faintness, as well as severe migraines which might leave her incapacitated for several days at a time. The only remedy she would ever take was chloroform. Although she always did her best to make light of it and carry on as normally as possible, as the ailments became more acute, she had to modify her schedule. When she could not be present at official functions because of illness, her place was taken by her sister Louise Sophie.

● ● ● ● ●

The deaths of Queen Victoria and the Empress Frederick had if anything reinforced her antipathy towards all things English, and strengthened her resolve to be as moral and pious as she was convinced the English royal family, presided over by the pleasure-loving King Edward VII, was emphatically not.

In November 1902 the Emperor was invited to Sandringham on a private visit for King Edward's sixty-first birthday, but the Empress did not accompany him. 'My mother is always in a fever if I or my father go to England,' the Crown Prince scoffed. Daisy, Princess of Pless, remarked that the Empress 'must have an extra supply of breath to enable her to gasp at her fantastic notions of all the horrible temptations that her husband and son have to resist in the dangerous little island; poor dear, she looks more like the Emperor's mother than his wife.'[4] As the Emperor remarked to Bernhard von Bülow in 1908, 'my wife has a fanatical hate for the English majesties'.[5] The Empress did not like it if her husband or sons stayed for more than a few days in England if she was not present. Apart from her intense Anglophobia, another of her reasons was that she feared that there were too many temptations in the form of the opposite sex.

Devoted to her sons, she was ambivalent about seeing them growing up and choosing wives for themselves. However, the Crown Prince proved something of an unwelcome throwback to his Hanoverian forebears in showing a rather precocious awareness of the opposite sex from childhood. In September 1890, when he was only eight, she had told Count Waldersee of her anxiety about the development of her eldest son and how he appeared to be showing a rather unhealthy interest in the opposite sex. Even at that age he could distinguish between pretty and ugly women, paid a disturbing amount of attention to the ladies' dresses, and was particularly polite and attentive towards the prettier ones.[6] While he was on a visit to England in 1901, eleven years later, he had taken a strong liking to the French-born American socialite Gladys Deacon, later the mistress and eventually wife of the 9th Duke of Marlborough and gave her a ring, which she was later ordered to return to him on the insistence of the angry Emperor.

Fearing that he might take after his great-uncle Bertie, King Edward VII, the Empress was keen to see her firstborn married as soon as possible. In June 1904 he was among the guests at the wedding of Frederick Francis IV, Grand Duke of Mecklenburg-Schwerin and Princess Alexandra of Hanover in Gmunden, and while he was there he met the groom's sister Cecilie for the first time. The two young people took a liking to each other, which soon deepened, and in September their engagement was officially announced. The wedding was due to take place in the spring or early summer next year, but had to be postponed for a fortnight because the Empress slipped on a staircase while she was staying at Wiesbaden, and fractured her arm.

It was accordingly held in Berlin on 6 June 1905. The festivities began two days earlier when Cecilie, accompanied by the Empress, rode into Berlin in the gold carriage of the Prussian kings, a vehicle which was used only on occasions of major importance. They took the traditional route through the Brandenburg Gate, and as they rode down Unter den Linden, thousands of well-wishers threw roses at them. On the morning of the wedding, the Empress accompanied Cecilie in a gold state landau from Potsdam into Berlin. Immediately before the ceremony, she placed the glistening Prussian bridal crown on the princess's head. At the conclusion, the bride and groom knelt to receive the blessing of the Emperor and Empress. As the latter embraced Cecilie, kissing her on each cheek, she turned to her son to tell him what a good choice of wife he had made.

The Crown Princess soon became very fond of her mother-in-law. She and her husband spent many a happy teatime in the palace where they would sit together by the fireside. Here they would have lengthy and absorbing conversations 'on all the questions that intimately concern a wife and mother, and I gained a growing insight into the soul of this woman, unique and unforgettable, in whom the family found its natural centre.'[7] The Empress doubtless had a great deal of sympathy for her, for much as she loved her sons, she was all too aware that her womanising eldest was never going to be a shining example of fidelity, and knew that any wife of his would need to exercise considerable forbearance. The Crown Princess was also happy to join her mother-in-law in taking part in promoting charitable causes. However Cecilie soon found there were difficulties in establishing a relationship with her mother-in-law, who was often too absorbed in her domestic duties to provide the close friendship for which the younger and sometimes lonely woman craved.

At the wedding the second of the princes, Eitel Frederick, had met Sophie Charlotte of Oldenburg, fallen in love with her, and in October 1905 their engagement was announced. Like his eldest brother the prince was a notorious womaniser, and his parents had long been concerned by the rumours that were circulating about him. The Empress even encouraged Oscar, who was by this time serving in the Prussian army, to avoid visiting Potsdam too often when he was home as she feared the elder brother could easily be a corrupting influence on the younger. Once again the only remedy, his parents were convinced, was for the young man to be married as soon as reasonably possible.

Nobody was ever under any illusions that this might have been a love match. 'Lotte' had spent most of her life under the eye of her stepmother, Elizabeth, Grand Duchess of Oldenburg, from whose stifling guardianship the young and marriageable spinster was most eager to escape. The prospect of marrying into the Prussian royal family seemed a good way out. However, within a few weeks of the wedding it was evident that this union was not going to be a happy one. He continued his affairs with other women, leaving his wife to occupy herself at her castle at Tiergarten while she painted, read, and entertained close friends.

Just as she adored her children, the Empress was also devoted to her grandchildren. Always good with small children, she would regularly make an effort to try and be present at the confinements of her daughters-in-law, and her presence in the delivery room was said to be soothing and reassuring. The youngsters were invited regularly to tea at the Neue Palais, and these afternoons were free from formality, when she seemed happy surrounded by lively grandsons, with no ladies-in-waiting or servants standing by. For once she would let down her guard and be totally at ease.

When Crown Prince and Princess Ferdinand of Roumania were visiting the family in 1910, the latter left a telling portrait of the woman who was her cousin by marriage. 'There was nothing really hearty about her,' Marie recorded in her memoirs some years later; 'she could never put off that attitude of stereotyped graciousness which too much resembled condescension to be quite pleasant.' However she conceded that the Empress was at her best and most relaxed when she was with her sons; 'in their company she lost some of her stiffness and of that shallow amiability which prevented any warmer intercourse.' When the princes crowded round her, evidently delighted to be in the company of a family member whom they rarely saw, they were fascinated by her orange shoes and stockings. They called the Empress to come and have a look, and the Crown Princess had to put her toes up on a sofa and pull a few inches of her long sweeping skirt to give them a good view. The Empress was rather taken aback by such unconventional attire, but 'carried away by the general gaiety she for a moment forgot to be condescending, and we all laughed heartily'. It was the only time Marie ever remembered seeing her behave really naturally. 'so to say off her guard and not acting.'[8]

In February 1906 the Emperor and Empress celebrated their silver wedding anniversary. As the exact day coincided with that of their son's wedding, they postponed their celebrations for a few days. The official celebrations in Prussia were appropriately grand, with King Edward VII sending his brother-in-law Prince Christian as his personal representative. On 26 February they received deputations from the Reichstag and other government officials offering their best wishes. After twenty-five years the marriage was still strong, and as they became older they became more devoted to each other. As events would soon prove, the Emperor relied on his wife a good deal more as the years went on, ironically in view of the fact that he had regarded her as little more than a broodhen at the beginning. In time she would prove the stronger of the two, and arguably at the expense of her personal health.

To his uncle Frederick, Grand Duke of Baden, he wrote in March that for him the best part of the celebrations was 'to see how rightly the people have judged the worth and the work of their Kaiserin, in full appreciation of what the Lord has also bestowed on them in her.'[9]

Some four months later, in July, Crown Princess William gave birth to their first grandchild. He was named William after his father and grandfather. At the time, the Crown Prince and Princess were living at the Marble Palace until their new home the Cecilienhof Palace could be completed. When the baby was about to be born the Crown Prince was on a hunting trip with friends. He returned home with some reluctance when word was sent that his wife was going into labour. Once the baby was born, he could not wait to get back to more convivial company as soon as he could, leaving his mother to support and nurse his wife.[10]

In 1906 allegations of homosexuality were made against Count Philipp zu Eulenburg, the Emperor's friend of many years. Their close companionship had irritated the Empress for many years. She was doubtless aware that her husband was in the habit of having long and confidential conversations with him, notably about their marital difficulties. The public exposure of his liaisons, which had apparently been going on before and after his marriage, led to his trial for perjury after he had denied any impropriety, but court proceedings were repeatedly postponed and ultimately never completed because of his ill-health. Nevertheless the Emperor could no longer publicly maintain their friendship. It had long been a barrier between husband and wife, and the Empress was undoubtedly relieved to see him forcibly retired from public life.

● ● ● ● ●

In November 1907 the Emperor and Empress paid a state visit to Britain. Although in the past he had often been very enthusiastic about returning to the country, this time he tried to get out of it by offering the excuse that he was suffering from bronchitis. King Edward VII sent him a telegram begging him to reconsider his decision. He knew that the King's telegram was an attempt to discredit him diplomatically, so he had no choice but to relent. The

Empress had planned to stay behind on the grounds that she was nursing her daughter Victoria Louise through chickenpox, but when the princess showed some improvement the Empress decided she could hardly avoid accompanying her husband after all. Such circumstances were not the most auspicious overture to their arrival.

On reaching Victoria Station they were met by George, Prince of Wales. The high point of their visit later that week was a drive by the couple through the streets of central London from Paddington Station to the Guildhall on 13 November. They were guests of honour at a reception at Mansion House, and the Emperor's speech at luncheon was enthusiastically received. At Windsor both expressed themselves 'enchanted' with their visit and everything went smoothly, though Charles Hardinge at the Foreign Office felt that it had been overshadowed by the publication of the German naval estimates which cast some doubt on the Emperor's assurances of peace and goodwill towards England in his recent speeches.

There were several other members of European royalty at Windsor at the same time, among them the King's youngest daughter Maud, Queen of Norway, Queen Amelie of Portugal, and King Alfonso XIII and Queen Victoria Eugenie of Spain. However it was observed that the haughty Empress appeared to make no effort whatsoever to be friendly with the other sovereign ladies.

After the visit was over the Empress went to the Netherlands to meet Queen Wilhelmina, while the Emperor went to relax at Highcliffe Castle, home of Colonel Edward Stuart-Wortley. One of the reasons for his wishing to stay there was that it was near the family home of Admiral Victor Montagu, who was not only known for his pro-German views but also the father of Mary Montagu, whom the Emperor had met in the summer of 1905 and by whom he had been somewhat entranced. He had every hope of being able to see Mary again, and whether their relationship was purely platonic or not is uncertain, but like his 'uncle Bertie', the Emperor still had an eye for an attractive woman. Around this time he was also making voyages around the Mediterranean, partly for the purpose of visiting another female companion, the Venetian Countess Annina Morosini. His acquaintance with both women had not passed unnoticed and it led to furious outbursts of jealousy from the Empress. She may have suspected him of infidelity and must have begun to wonder whether her husband, like their eldest son, was starting to take after King Edward VII.

Before leaving for Germany, the Emperor suggested to Admiral Montagu that their table-talk might be written up into a newspaper article, which would enlighten British readers as to his policies and above all his friendly feelings towards Britain. It would however turn out to be one of the worst, most badly thought-out moves he would ever make.

- 6 -

The last years of peace, 1908-14

On 22 October 1908 there was a third marriage within the children, namely that of the Emperor and Empress's third son Augustus William to his first cousin Alexandra Victoria of Schleswig-Holstein, daughter of the Empress's younger sister Caroline Matilda, now Duchess. The ceremony took place on the same day as the Empress's fiftieth birthday. At the wedding banquet, the Emperor delivered an effusive address in praise of the bride, whom he welcomed as a true helper of her aunt and her mother-in-law the Empress. Yet not for the first time within the family, the marriage was not to prove a happy one. Within a few weeks the princess was earning a reputation for appearing sarcastic and snide to those around him, while her husband was plainly discontented with his lot.

Meanwhile, the text of the conversations that the Emperor had had with Colonel Stuart-Wortley, now promoted to the rank of brigadier, the previous year was about to find its way into print. During the summer the officer had been invited to attend the army manoeuvres at Metz. After further meetings with the Emperor, he wrote up the remarks in the form of an article and sent it to him with the suggestion that it could be used to secure 'a fair hearing' for Germany in the British press. Among other things, it said that Queen Victoria had appealed to him for advice during the Boer war, and that in agreement with his general staff he recommended a particular strategy which the British troops had followed with success; that there would be eventual war between the United States and Japan, and how he was building up the German fleet partly in order to 'be ready to end a helping hand' against the 'Yellow Peril' if necessary; and that he was Britain's greatest friend abroad, the one man capable of holding back the anti-British sentiments of his subjects in Germany. In spite of this, he complained that he was cruelly misunderstood and regarded as an arch-enemy by the English, who were 'as mad as March hares'.

Somehow, the finished copy escaped official vetting, and it was published word for word in the *Daily Telegraph* on 28 October 1908. The result was uproar in both countries, and it culminated in what would be the worst peacetime crisis of his reign.

It had followed the disgrace of Eulenburg, whom the Empress had never liked, on suspicion of being involved in homosexual practices. Worse still, it coincided with the black farce of an episode at a stag party which the Emperor had attended, when Count Dietrich von Hülsen-Haseler, chief of the imperial military cabinet, performed his regular party piece as a ballerina, suitably attired in a ballet dress. He then promptly collapsed and died of a heart attack, and rigor mortis set in before he could be removed from his tutu and dressed in his normal clothes again. Everybody present was at pains to prevent anyone else from knowing that one of his most respected servants had met his maker while performing for him in drag. All this, coming on top of the embarrassment of the *Daily Telegraph* 'interview', happened at the worst possible time.

Unable to cope with this procession of disasters, next month the devastated Emperor took to his bed. Voices in the Reichstag were calling for his abdication, and the Crown Prince assured everyone he was ready to succeed his father. Family and government, who regarded him as even less capable than his father, thought it was a case of 'better the devil you know'.

On 17 November Bülow came to Potsdam for a private meeting with the Emperor and Empress. As he approached on the terrace, the Empress came forward to him and whispered, 'Be really kind and gentle with the Emperor. He is quite broken up.'[1] The chancellor and a very pale, dejected-looking sovereign had a long conversation which touched on several topics, in the course of which the former tactfully advised him that they would 'win through' as long as His Majesty made up his mind to be more cautious and discreet in future.

Yet the worst was not over for the imperial couple. Two days later, Bülow had just risen to his feet to make a speech in the Reichstag when one of his staff came to his side and whispered that he had been given a telephone message to say that His Majesty intended to abdicate. After he had left the building and was strolling outside, a man whom he recognised as one of the footmen came running towards him and handed him a letter, addressed in the Empress's handwriting. Inside was a brief letter, saying. 'I should like to speak to you. The messenger will tell you the rest.'

He made straight for the Neue Palais where the Empress received him on the ground floor. With a regal bearing, but her eyes red, she asked him immediately, 'Must the Emperor abdicate? 'Do you wish him to abdicate?' He assured the Empress that such a thing had never occurred to him, and he could not see the slightest necessity for it. She asked him to sit down, and then told him that her husband had had 'a nervous breakdown'. It had happened before, she said, after moments of emotional crisis, but this time it was more serious and he had taken to his bed. The chancellor replied that he was fully convinced the storm would blow itself out, but it would be necessary for His Majesty to be more discreet and moderate in his general attitude. When the meeting was finished and she dismissed the chancellor, she seemed calmer.[2]

Over the next few days the Empress helped to repair William's frayed nerves and restored something of his old self-confidence. Though during their early married life he had treated his wife as little more than a child, through the years he had come to depend on her as one of the few people he could trust. Now, the transformation became complete. If he had not actually had a complete breakdown he was perilously close to one, but with care and a lack of further excitement he was soon restored to something approaching his old self. Though he might never quite be the same man as before, and though he never really recovered his previous self-esteem, at least her calming influence prevented him from sliding into complete dejection, as well as providing him with a shoulder to lean on.

It was ironic that William had married a wife who he thought at the time 'knew her place' and would not attempt to exert a fraction of the influence on her husband that her two predecessors had over the previous German Emperors. For it was this crisis which had the effect of convincing the Empress that she needed to involve herself more in the political affairs of the German empire. It was her opinion that Bülow should be retained as chancellor. Although she knew better than to make her views known, she secretly agreed with many that he could hardly be blamed for the Emperor's naivety and folly in speaking so freely and thus being responsible as much as anybody else for the *Daily Telegraph* affair.

Always ready to blame somebody else, the Emperor was furious that his chancellor had not suppressed or edited the 'interview', but the position of Bülow was one subject on which Their Majesties would doubtless have had to agree to differ. His position had been gravely weakened, although he continued in office until the summer of 1909. After being defeated in the Reichstag on difficulties in obtaining additional finance for ongoing ship construction and failure to carry a majority for imposing inheritance taxes, he offered his resignation in June 1909.

A fortnight later he and his wife were received in farewell audience by the Empress. She told him how much she deplored and regretted his retirement, telling him that if she had had her way, he would have remained in his position for another twenty years. He replied with a gentle smile that His Majesty the Emperor would not have found an eighty-year-old Chancellor much use. With a note of anxiety, she asked for his reassurance that he would not make any speeches in the Reichstag against the Emperor. As he kissed her hand, he promised that as a loyal monarchist he would never create any difficulties for him. She then said that she had 'nearly always' felt in agreement with him, and that in only two matters had she been unable to share his opinion. One was about the Death Duties Bill, which he had proposed and which she thought would ruin the nobility, the support of altar and throne, and at the same time destroy family life. The other was that she thought he had been too friendly to England, a country which she believed was not to be trusted.[3]

On Bülow's advice, the Emperor reluctantly appointed Theobald von Bethmann-Hollweg, imperial state secretary for the interior, as his successor. Neither the Emperor nor the Empress were particularly enthusiastic about him as a person, or his fitness for office. The Empress considered that he was 'too philosophical, unworldly and ponderous' as well as having an uncongenial personality.[4] Nevertheless, Bülow's recommendation was accepted and his successor took office as chancellor in July.

In view of the fact that at the start of their married life the Empress had been seen as the personification of the good German *Hausfrau* whose only concerns were *Kirche, Küche, Kinder,* it is surprising to learn that in the early years of the twentieth century she became supportive of the right of women to vote. This was in stark contrast to the views of her husband, who regarded the British suffragettes with unconcealed contempt, declaring that they deserved a good flogging. In a speech at Königsberg in 1910, he declared that the principal duty of German women lay not 'in the acquisition of alleged rights through which they might become equal to men, but rather in the quiet work of the household and the family.' It was their business to educate the younger generation, 'especially in obedience and respect for their elders.'[5]

● ● ● ● ●

After George V succeeded his father Edward VII as King of Great Britain in May 1910, he suggested that the Emperor ought to come to London one year later for the unveiling of the memorial to their grandmother in front of Buckingham Palace. William, Augusta Victoria and their daughter Victoria Louise spent three days in London; they were pleasantly surprised to find such a friendly atmosphere at Buckingham Palace, and that England, her people, monarch, and government appeared more well-disposed towards Germany than they had dared to hope. However, it proved to be the last time that they ever visited England.

Shortly before leaving Berlin, the Emperor raised the delicate question of Morocco with King George V. It was a hurried exchange, and when he was back in Berlin he assured Bethmann-Hollweg that the King would never wage a war for the sake of that particular territory. Following a rebellion in Morocco against the Sultan that spring, the French had sent a small force to restore law and order, ostensibly to protect European lives and property. In June the Spanish army occupied two towns in Morocco and three weeks later a German gunboat, *Panther*, arrived at the port of Agadir under the pretext of protecting German trade interests. There was an immediate reaction from the French and the British, with the latter anxious to restrain France from adopting hasty measures and to dissuade her from sending troops to Fez, but without success. The British, worried by *Panther's* arrival, were convinced that the Germans meant to turn Agadir into a naval base on the Atlantic, and accordingly sent battleships to North Africa in case war broke out.

With Germany suddenly plunged into financial turmoil after the stock market fell and there was a run on the banks, the Emperor backed down and let the French take over most of Morocco. The German ambassador in Paris informed the French government that Germany had no territorial aspirations there and would negotiate for a French protectorate on the basis of compensation for Germany in the French Congo and the safeguarding of her economic interests. The German terms, as presented a week later, while containing an offer to cede additional territory elsewhere in Africa, demanded from France large areas of the French Congo. A speech on 21 July by David Lloyd George, the British Chancellor of the Exchequer, in which he declared that national honour was more precious than peace, was interpreted by Germany as a warning that she could not impose an unreasonable settlement on France.

With this Europe seemed closer to war than at any time for several decades, and the Emperor and his ministers were surprised by the reaction from London, as they had expected the British government to acquiesce, rather than treating the matter as a grave threat to peace. The Empress urged her husband to take an unbending militaristic line with the British and French, lest accusations be made later that a Hohenzollern 'had bowed to these opponents and backed down'.[6] In November Germany recognised France's right to 'protect' Morocco, receiving in exchange a certain amount of the French Congo.

Yet tension between Britain and France on one hand and Germany on the other had increased as a result. While the Emperor might equivocate in his attitude towards Britain, the Empress never would. In March 1912, when the Emperor and his ministers were embroiled again with Anglo-German negotiations on naval strength, the Empress went to see Bethmann-Hollweg and urged him 'not to give way to England'.[7]

●●●●●

At this stage, three of the imperial princes were already married. The next of the siblings to go would be Victoria Louise, known in the family as Sissy. She had inherited her mother's dignity, carriage and grace, and also an imperious, wilful streak from her father. The youngest of seven children, she knew that she was the only one of whom her father was really fond, and he often indulged her although he was unfailingly firm with his sons. Her flippant attitude caused many a disagreement between her mother and herself. There was something of a generation gap, with the Empress's very decided and old-fashioned opinions on propriety which led her into clashes with her daughter. Once when the latest Paris fashions had arrived in Germany, the Empress complained about how inappropriate she considered the latest unnaturally short slit skirts. Only a few days later, Sissy and her sister-in-law Cecilie scandalised the Empress by walking into a room wearing two of these skirts, merely in order to shock her.

In 1912 Ernest Augustus of Hanover came to Berlin after the death of his elder brother George in a car crash. The latter had been on his way to Denmark in May to attend the funeral of his uncle, King Frederick VIII of Denmark, when his car skidded off the road near Nackel in Brandenburg. The Emperor insisted that Crown Prince William and Eitel Frederick should comprise part of the guard of honour that escorted the body to its final resting place.

Ernest Augustus came to Berlin to meet the Emperor and thank him in person for his gesture of sympathy in sending his sons to take part in such an occasion. Dressed in his light blue uniform of the Bavarian military, Ernest Augustus was invited to an audience with the Empress, who was greatly impressed by him. She commented how pleasant it was to see a Bavarian uniform, which looked just like the one in which her father went to war in 1870. She also felt a certain affinity for the family because, like her own family, they had been dispossessed during Bismarck's military expansion of Prussia. As for Sissy, he was smitten by her and she was very taken by him. Nevertheless several political issues had to be overcome, and required the help of most of the princess's brothers and her sister-in-law Cecilie.

When the betrothal was certain, the Empress was thrilled. She wedding was set for 24 May 1913, an auspicious date in the history of the family as it had been the birthday of Queen Victoria. There was a great deal of etiquette to be observed, and as the princess would later recall, they were constantly beset by people, especially by ladies-in-waiting and court officials, wanting to give advice concerning the princess's wedding. The Empress was responsible for shouldering the responsibility of planning the wedding, arrangements, but all the unwanted and unsolicited suggestions made her task an arduous one, not to say stressful. Ernest Augustus had great sympathy with her in the situation, and before the wedding he wrote to Sissy to say how angry he was with the ladies at court, who were greatly to blame for making her so nervous. When it was remembered that none of them were married, he added, how could they want to involve themselves in such business?

Among the guests who gathered in Berlin for the wedding were King George V, Queen Mary, Tsar Nicholas II (arriving in an armoured train, for reasons of security, and not accompanied this time by the increasingly unwell Tsarina), and the bride's great-aunt Louise, Dowager Duchess of Baden. A civil ceremony was held in the Electress's Hall, and the religious ceremony in the chapel. It was remarked that Augusta Victoria looked one of the best-dressed of the guests that day, wearing a light green robe-style dress adorned with long strings of pearls and a diamond-encrusted crown. The banquets and gala operas, military parades and other trappings of imperial German splendour that preceded it were witnessed by the last great congregation of family and European royalty. Few of them could have realised that they would never see each other again.

The Empress was totally bereft after the marriage of her youngest child. When the bride and groom changed their clothes and went to the station for the start of their honeymoon, four of her brothers as well as their father accompanied them. Adalbert and Oscar stayed at the palace with her, as she was taking the moment of parting very badly and could not bear to go but at the same time, it was felt, she ought not to be left alone. That same day she closed the book which she had begun to keep after her daughter's birth, with the words,

> I shall say nothing about myself, except that it seemed that heart was breaking. I could only pray, particularly as I knelt at my child's bed during the night, God protect my child, my youngest. Make her happy, O Lord.[8]

On the day after the wedding, the Empress invited the princess's former governess, Anne Topham, to dinner. Since her engagement, the Empress told her, 'the poor child did nothing but cry'. She was convinced that war would break out, her husband would go away to fight and they would never see each other again. The court physician, Dr Zunker, tried to reassure her that even if there was to be war in the Balkans, he was certain that it would all be over within six weeks.[9]

• • • • •

The following month saw celebrations for the silver jubilee of the accession of the Emperor. Over the weekend of 14-15 June, Berlin was *en fête*, the streets decorated with jubilee arches bearing the imperial cypher and flags fluttering everywhere. The Hohenzollern family assembled together in Berlin, and there were productions at the Schloss theatre of Josef Lauff's *Der Grosse König*, with music by Frederick the Great, and of Wagner's *Lohengrin*. On 16 June, the actual jubilee day, there was a morning serenade by Berlin schoolchildren in the courtyard of the Schloss, with deputations marching past. It was all too much for the Empress, who had not been on the best of health for a while. At the banquet that night, she collapsed and had to be taken to her rooms. The Emperor likewise seemed unable to join in the festive mood. In addition to anxiety about his wife's health, friends thought that he was suffering from depression as a result of his daughter's marriage and also missing her badly.

The Empress's health, it was said, seemed to suffer further as a result of her daughter's leaving home, and she pined for her companionship. She was however soon distracted by the betrothal and imminent wedding of one of her godchildren, her namesake Princess Augusta Victoria. Born in 1890, she was the daughter of William, Prince of Hohenzollern, the brother of Crown Prince Ferdinand of Romania. It was believed that the Empress would have liked her goddaughter to have married one of her sons, but two difficulties stood in the way. The young Augusta Victoria did not like any of these distant cousins, and in any case, her branch of the family were strict Roman Catholics.[10] Nevertheless the Empress took a keen interest in her forthcoming marriage to Manuel, the former King of Portugal, who had been forced to abdicate his throne in 1910 following a republican uprising in his doomed kingdom.

This wedding had caused no controversy, but the same could not be said of the nuptials for the fifth son of the Emperor and Empress, Oscar, who had had the temerity to fall in love with a commoner. He had met Countess Ina von Bassewitz-Levetzow, after the wedding of the Crown Prince. The Empress had taken an instant liking to her, and appointed her one of her ladies-in-waiting. Within a few months, the latter had helped to fill the void in the Empress's life that had been left after her daughter had married and moved away. She was won over by the endearing awkwardness and quiet personality of Oscar, who had grown up to be a more likeable young man than his frequently loud and conceited brothers.

For princes who fell in love with ladies-in-waiting, the road to matrimony was never a smooth one. They kept their relationship a secret at first, but one evening Eitel Frederick, probably rather the worse for drink, attacked Ina. Oscar heard her screaming, came running to find out what was going on, and in his anger knocked his brother on to the floor. As he tried to calm Ina down, he declared to his mother that he loved Ina, and intended to marry her. If he was forbidden to do so, then he would make her his wife anyway and they were prepared to go into exile.

She had long suspected that there had been some kind of attachment between them both. Fully conscious of the family's reputation, it would have been very unlike her to have agreed to any of her sons making a morganatic marriage, as she was known to be as obsessive as anybody else of her generation with regard to morganatic marriages. However Oscar had always been a particular favourite of hers, and she felt there was no good reason to oppose the marriage for the sake of time-honoured tradition. He was one of the younger sons, with no chance of succeeding to the throne; and it was clear than he had made his mind up. She accordingly asked the Emperor for permission for them to marry, and it came as little surprise to her when his initial reaction was to lose his temper. He told her that it was sheer folly on his part even to consider the very idea, and insisted that Ina should be given one hour to clear out of Berlin and never to return.

Ina accordingly obeyed, but she was prepared to be patient and hope that her sovereign would eventually relent. The Empress and Oscar argued and pleaded with the Emperor for several weeks to give his consent to the marriage, and at length their opposition wore him down. The Duchess of Brunswick, who agreed wholeheartedly with them, added her support. Her first child was about to be christened, and when her father asked her what she would like him to give her for a present, she said that all she really wanted was permission for her brother Oscar to be allowed to marry the love of his life. He conceded, and the engagement was publicly announced on 26 May.

News that one of the Emperor's sons was about to contract a morganatic marriage created some disquiet within the family. The prince's aunt, now Princess Adolf of Schaumburg-Lippe, who almost thirty years earlier as the young spinster Princess Victoria had been bitterly ostracised by her eldest brother when she wanted to marry one of the Battenberg princes descended from a morganatic marriage, must have been particularly astonished. Eitel Frederick was especially hostile to the match, but as far as the family was concerned he found himself in a minority. At last they realised that times and attitudes were changing.

Yet the Emperor, Empress and their relations were quite unaware just how great the changes about to take place would be. The war, which some of them had foreseen, would be more prolonged than any of the other conflicts the Emperor and Empress had yet lived through. It would have an incalculable effect not just on their lives, but also on the monarchies of Europe in general.

- 7 -

The First World War, 1914-18

On 20 June 1914, the Emperor departed on his yacht *Hohenzollern* for Hamburg to be present at the christening of a new liner. A couple of days later he went to Kiel for a sailing regatta which was also attended by several British and German pleasure boats, and a squadron from the Royal Navy. As he had a feeling that the British contingent were intending to find out naval or military secrets, he requested the presence of detectives, and gave orders that foreign guests were to be kept off his ships. However, there were no difficulties or incidents, and he commented afterwards that he was pleased as ever with the sense of comradeship and hospitality that his ships had enjoyed when meeting the Royal Navy.

The Empress and her sons were conspicuous by their absence from the Kiel regatta. While they did not normally attend, this year it was rumoured that they had deliberately stayed away as they hated England so much and were contemptuous of what they saw as the Emperor's excessive fraternisation with the British officers and squadron. However, his participation in the regatta was about to be drawn to an orderly but swift conclusion. On the afternoon of 28 June, he was racing in his yacht *Meteor* when the head of his naval cabinet received an urgent telegram informing him that Archduke Francis Ferdinand, heir to the throne of Austria-Hungary, and his wife Sophie had been assassinated that morning on a visit to Sarajevo, the capital of Bosnia.

Just over a month later, what some of the more far-sighted had feared for a long time came to pass. On 31 July, the German ambassador in Moscow was informed that total Russian mobilisation had taken place the night before, and the Emperor ordered a full mobilisation of German forces. To the end, he still hoped that Britain would remain neutral, as telegrams between the nations arrived and were sent. The Empress seemed resigned, even eager, to see Britain ranged with Germany's enemies, saying that war was the only thing left, and her husband and six sons would be going off to it.[1]

Oscar, who had been engaged for three months, was about to take up his army command and most of those at court, including his brother Eitel Frederick who had been particularly hostile to his engagement, wanted to have him sent out join his regiment immediately. As regards the matter of his marriage, the time to act was now, and Ina was summoned back to Berlin that same day. Preparations were made as quickly as possible, and a small private wedding was held that night at Bellevue Palace, attended by the Emperor and Empress. He would not create his daughter-in-law a princess, but instead he conferred on her the title of Countess von Ruppin, which gave her greater precedence at court.

On 1 August, Germany declared war on Russia. Two days later, the German empire declared war on France, and that same day there was the second imperial wedding within the family in a week, when Adalbert married his second cousin, Adelaide of Saxe-Meiningen, whom he had been courting for several years. The groom was a lieutenant on board SMS *Luitpold*, which was at the naval base of Wilhelmshaven in Schleswig-Holstein. When he was informed that war was imminent, like his brother Oscar, he decided that he and Adelaide ought to be married as soon as possible. A simple military wedding was held in the chapel at the naval base on 3 August, attended by a few officers and performed by the chaplain at Wilhelmshaven.

On the following day, Great Britain declared war on Germany. The Emperor and Empress were at the Neue Palais, and in a display of patriotic fervour and to show unity with the empire, the imperial family made the journey in cars to the Stadtschloss in Berlin, as cheering people in their thousands took to the streets. It was noticed that some of them, particularly the Crown Prince and Princess, were nodding and smiling occasionally to acknowledge the crowds, but the Emperor's face was a mask, neither betraying the merest look at his subjects around him, nor even the flicker of a smile. When they arrived back at the palace, the Emperor, Empress and Crown Prince all came out on the balcony, where the crowds were still cheering. The Emperor spoke briefly, to tell them that all political parties now ceased and they were all brothers.

Yet it seemed that that most of the cheers were for the Empress, who was the most popular, best loved member of the family. It had been her unpretentious upbringing and simple, traditional values which enabled the German people to feel personally connected with her in a way which they could not with the Emperor.

As for their reactions to the outbreak of war, the Emperor was furious at what he saw as British betrayal of his persistent attempts at friendship. He asked rhetorically how the British could have forgotten their brotherhood when they had fought together against France at Waterloo less than a century earlier. However, the Empress ranted with passion and anger against the enemies of Germany, reminding him that she had long predicted the outbreak of war which had now become reality.[2]

● ● ● ● ●

When Emperor William left for the front on 12 August, the Empress wrote him a letter of reassurance:

> But God will bring you back to me in good health, that is what you must always tell yourself whenever your poor nerves and your poor heart feel so depressed. Then you must always remember that I sense it from afar, [and] even though I cannot be with you, in my prayers I am always close to you and will try to calm you. – Don't take it all so much to heart, my darling, you can face the world with a clear conscience. Your country is fighting calmly for its holiest values and the Lord will show it the way forward...[3]

Now Germany and her Austro-Hungarian ally were at war with Britain, any respect and admiration the Emperor and Empress might have felt for their ruling cousins, now their enemies, King George and Queen Mary in Britain, and Tsar Nicholas and Empress Alexandra in Russia, soon evaporated. Augusta Victoria's American dentist Dr Arthur Davis believed that she was profoundly affected by the gravity of what was happening, and bitterly opposed to the war. Yet once the fighting had broken out, she was busier than ever, doing all she could for the war effort. As *Landesmutter* or mother of the country, she was tireless in visiting hospitals, and wounded soldiers welcomed visits from her almost as much as they did from their own mothers. At the same time she made an appeal to the women of Germany to step up and assume their positions as contributing members of society at such a difficult time.

> The struggle will be gigantic and the wounds to be healed innumerable. Therefore, I call upon you women and girls of

Germany, and upon all to whom it is not given to fight for our beloved home, for help. Let everyone now do what lies in her power to lighten the struggle for our husbands, sons and brothers. I know that in all ranks of our people without exception the will exists to discharge this high duty, but may the Lord God strengthen us in our holy work of love, which summons us women to devote all our strength to the Fatherland in its decisive struggle.[4]

● ● ● ● ●

During the first few months of the war, the German military machine looked perfectly effective, if not quite invincible. In February 1915 German forces drove the Russians out of East Prussia, and thanksgiving services were held in churches across Berlin. The Emperor, Empress and Duke of Brunswick attended a special service in Berlin Cathedral, and the sovereigns were enthusiastically cheered when they went to the church. The Emperor was naturally able to bask in the reflected glory from his generals, who were responsible for all successes. Soon after the war began, he had been forced to surrender his powers as supreme warlord of the German military to the Chief of General Staff, Helmuth von Moltke. The Empress was aghast when she learned that Moltke had stripped her husband of his prerogatives, and turned him into a mere figurehead representing the German war effort. It was not long before he had little if anything to do with the day-to-day combat planning.

As food rationing and fuel shortages throughout Germany became more prevalent, the petitions that the Empress received from charities, church parishes and hospitals increased. The Emperor was at headquarters, and she now found herself becoming the public face of the monarchy at home. She moved her family out from the Stadtschloss into Bellevue Palace, which enabled her to save money on utilities, staff and general maintenance costs. She saw it as her responsibility to set an example for a less lavish lifestyle during the war, and anything that savoured of luxury was banished from the table.

According to her sister-in-law Victoria, Princess Adolf of Schaumburg-Lippe, throughout the war years she was always the first to sacrifice herself to her country, and to encourage others to do likewise. When certain ladies in society continued to throw grand parties 'with delicacies heaped on their tables', the Empress reprimanded them for entertaining in such style when so many hundreds of people were starving.[5] Moving to Bellevue also enabled her to spend more time with the family of the Crown Prince, while he was commanding the Fifth Army.

She also kept a motherly eye on the families of her other sons. It was a particular source of sadness when Adalbert's wife Adelaide gave birth to a daughter on 4 September 1915, named Victoria Marina, a sickly baby who only lived for a few hours. Grief at the loss of this grandchild, the separation from her husband, and burdens imposed by the war soon began to take their toll on her health. Now aged fifty-six, she was beginning to fall prey to heart and back trouble, lack of sleep, and recurring moods of depression. Her hair had turned prematurely white a few years earlier, allegedly as a result of certain drugs she had been taking in her effort to avert a tendency to put on weight.[6]

With the war, she had to take on more tasks than ever before. Among them was her responsibility for managing the imperial residences, which at one point included almost sixty palaces and castles in the Berlin-Brandenburg region alone. At the same time she also had the burden of managing an increasingly unstable husband. Once he had lost his status as supreme warlord, with his chiefs of staff, his military cabinet and the generals making all the important decisions, he veered wildly between euphoria and low spirits. One moment he would demand that his soldiers take no prisoners, and next he would insist that if one German family starved because of the British blockade, he would send a Zeppelin over Windsor Castle to blow up the entire British royal family. Then he would be plunged back into a mood of depression and take sleeping pills.

Those who were closest to him, family and personal suite alike, were alarmed by his sudden changes in mood. The Empress insisted that he should be allowed plenty of rest, with his sleep uninterrupted unless there was urgent news. She and his adjutant, General von Plessen, told his suite that their first duty was to keep the Emperor in good spirits, protected from bad tidings and hardship as much as possible. German defeats were not mentioned to him, and he was only shown positive battle reports or given news of victories. He was briefed each day on the latest war news, but only on a selective basis and on plans that had already been carried out, but never informed of any forthcoming missions.

By 1916 the Emperor found himself relying on his wife more than ever. She was increasingly the strength behind the throne. In public, he propagated the myth of a powerful, confident *paterfamilias*, while she the role of the *kleines hausfrau*, but the truth was rather different. Behind his façade was a man plagued by insecurities and prone to emotional instability. The Empress had weathered her fair share of emotional storms in her life and became his rock. The days of hysteria and jealousy were gone, and in supporting her husband, she found a new strength and fortitude. In trying to make her husband's burden as light as possible, she kept in regular contact with his ministers.

At the same time she continued to maintain a simple domestic routine for her family in Berlin. She spent her evenings by the fireside, knitting clothes for soldiers, making arrangements to care for the wounded or the widowed, or taking tea with her ladies. When her husband returned from headquarters at Spa, she worked hard to entertain him and his entourage, keeping their spirits up whenever they appeared overtired or disheartened. However, much as he loved her and valued her influence, it was no secret that he preferred to spend his leisure time in the company of other men, be they soldiers, ministers or other princes. Moreover, although he was head of state and nominally commander-in-chief of the armed forces belonging to the empire's constituent states, a shift in power had come. Although he was slow to recognise the fact, the influence of 'the warlord of the Second Reich' had sharply diminished. For some time, power had been moving into the hands of the chief of general staff Paul von Hindenburg and his deputy Erich von Ludendorff, and in 1916 they threatened to resign unless the Emperor dismissed his chancellor Theobald von Bethmann-Hollweg. Now his generals had taken control of the day-to-day conduct of the war, he began to lose his grip on reality. In his more rational if embittered moments, he admitted that all he did was go for walks, drink tea, and saw wood – and nobody told him anything.

The Empress watched anxiously as he alternated between a sense of utter despair and deluded dreams of victory. It all added to her problems, since her own health was suffering and she was doing everything she could to take her mind off it, such as keeping a closer eye on children, with her sons involved in the fighting, alongside the rest of German manhood, and her grandchildren.

The youngest of her sons was about to become a further cause of considerable worry. Now aged twenty-five, the weak and outrageously spoilt Joachim was described by Countess Emilie Alsenborg, one of his mother's ladies-in-waiting, as not strong, 'either mentally or morally'. His military duties were never onerous, and he spent much of his time gambling, for want of anything better to do, and running up vast debts. He became personally involved with Erna, the sister of his equerry, Franz von Weberhardt, but his reasons were evidently less than romantic. On her nineteenth birthday her father had presented her with a magnificent collection of jewels which had been in the family for several generations, and she was wearing these when she initially met the prince. His creditors were becoming ever more pressing in their demands for payment, and he was afraid to ask his parents for financial assistance. On a visit to the Weberhardts' castle in Saxony, he begged Erna to let him have the jewellery so he could pledge them on a temporary basis in order to settle his debts, and on the understanding that he would return them. She handed them over, and he returned to Berlin where he immediately sold them instead.

At the time, the Empress had been involved in plans to arrange a marriage between him and Marie Augusta, the daughter of Prince Edward of Anhalt, later Duke all too briefly. Count von Zeppelin, a close friend of the Anhalt family, informed the Empress that he would tell them about the prince's disgraceful behaviour. She was deeply upset, as she feared that her son would be forced to marry Erna in order to keep the scandal quiet. (Erna would doubtless have been equally aghast at the very idea of having to marry someone who had so shamelessly reneged on his word, but as he was the son of the Emperor she would probably have been in little position to refuse). The price of his silence, the Count stipulated, would be for the Empress to do what she could to persuade the Emperor to consent to Zeppelin airship bombing raids over London, something which he was reluctant to do. She had no option but to agree, although as she now hated the British more than ever it is unlikely that she ever had second thoughts on the matter.

Meanwhile she confronted Joachim about his behaviour. The equally furious Weberhardts were duly informed where Erna's jewels had gone. As for the humiliated Joachim, fearful of what his father's reaction would be when he was told, he was left with no choice but to agree to visit the unfortunate Marie Augusta and propose to her.

The couple were married in March 1916, at a simple ceremony at Bellevue consisting of a Lutheran service with only a few guests. The Emperor, who may or may not have been informed at this stage about his son's misconduct, insisted that his duties at Spa were too pressing for him to return for a mere wedding and he could not be present. The Empress had forgiven Joachim, and mother and son were both deeply wounded by his father's absence.

At around the time of the ceremony, Irish republican leaders briefly considered offering the throne of an independent Ireland to Joachim. It never reached the stage of an informal invitation, but any King of Ireland would almost certainly have been required to be or become a Roman Catholic. The Catholic-hating Empress would have fiercely resented any of her children from thus changing their religion. A year later, there was talk of him being offered the throne of the independent Russian state of Georgia, but likewise nothing came of this.

German military leaders were now starting to perceive the hidden strengths of their Empress's personality. With six sons on the battlefield and the interests of her grandchildren at stake, as well as those of her husband, she was proving increasingly single-minded. Aware that her husband was apt to waver and prove indecisive, she was always ready to stiffen his resolve. Her advice to him was to pursue the British, whom she hated more and more as time went on, to insist on the forceful prosecution of the war on all fronts, and when the time came, to demand appropriate annexations of territory which would reward the Fatherland for the sacrifices it had made during war. She took it on herself to act as an intermediary between her husband, General Hindenburg, Admiral Tirpitz, General Gröner, and other major figures in order to win the Emperor's approval of their ideas or to keep them in his favour. One general who had previously regarded her as something of a nonentity remarked approvingly, 'Now that's a strong woman!'[7]

Less popular, perhaps, were her ever more frequent visits to her husband while he was at his headquarters. Much as the Emperor relished her company, some members of his entourage were angry that these appearances by her gave the lie to the image of the supreme war lord as a soldier King sharing the harsh conditions of his troops, which he plainly was not doing. As one of them lamented, 'the entire hero legend is fading fast!'[8] They were outraged by his sense of detachment when he seemed more interested in visiting art exhibitions, going for drives, continuing with his hobby of excavating archaeological remains and designing officers' rest homes, as if they were still at peace and somehow the fighting had nothing to do with him.

While the Emperor now hated Britain and the British with a new savagery, sometimes the Empress appeared to loathe them even more. In October 1915 King Alfonso XIII of Spain, a country which remained neutral throughout the conflict, asked her to intercede on behalf of Edith Cavell, an English nurse who had been arrested and court-martialled for helping some two hundred Allied soldiers escape from German-occupied Belgium, and sentenced to death. She refused, saying that women who behaved like men must be punished like men. Edith Cavell accordingly went bravely to her death in front of a German firing squad.

More than ever, the Emperor was inviting her to join in discussions with the political and military leaders on future policy, something which would have been unthinkable in the early months of their marriage. Ever since the resignation of Bülow, a year after the *Daily Telegraph* incident, she felt that German policy had been drifting into dangerously democratic waters, something which would weaken the prestige of the monarchy. For this she blamed the new Chancellor, Bethmann-Hollweg, and the Crown Prince agreed with her. In July 1917 when the chancellor asked the Emperor to concede equal suffrage to the Prussian lower house in the Reichstag, he agreed to summon a Crown Council to consider the question. Members of the council were divided, and the Emperor agreed to reserve his position. When he reported back to the Empress everything that had been discussed, she was furious. According to Rudolf von Valentini, chief of the civil cabinet, she had made 'a most terrible scene' which upset her husband so much that he spent a sleepless night in consequence.[9]

Bethmann-Hollweg resigned later that week and was succeeded by Georg Michaelis, who held power for only three months. Much to the anger of the Empress his successor, Count Georg von Hertling, was a Bavarian Roman Catholic from Bavaria when she would undoubtedly have much preferred a good Prussian Lutheran. As she became older she proved herself increasingly bigoted and resistant to change, and like her contemporary, the former Empress Alexandra of Russia, implacably opposed to any diminution of the power of the imperial crown. Her husband had been divinely appointed to rule, and rule he must. Valentini had proved a loyal and wise counsellor for several years, but the Empress and the Crown Prince held him responsible for what was seen as a lurch to the left in the Reichstag.[10] Finding his position increasingly untenable, under pressure he resigned in January 1918.

Long before the war was over, the Emperor was seen rightly or wrongly by many as the personification of utter villainy, the man who had started the war, and the one responsible for ordering the indiscriminate killing of women and children in Belgium and the destruction of whole towns and villages. Even in Germany he was blamed for leading the empire into a war which was proving too expensive, taking too long and costing too many lives. Conversely, the popularity of the Empress was increasing. Even though she was as reactionary in her political beliefs as him and took an uncompromising stand on the power of the monarch, she was seen as the one most concerned with the general welfare of Germans, particularly in her standing up for the well-being of the poorer classes.

Politicians and generals alike admired her handling of affairs during the war. As she had proved in 1908, moments of crisis which had proved too much for her increasingly volatile and neurotic husband brought out the best in her. In July 1918 his faith in his generals was beginning to waver, and she went to Headquarters at Spa, Belgium, in order to strengthen his resolve. More than ever she encouraged him to be the autocrat, to stand up to those around him whom she maintained would usurp his authority, and not to accept any demands from his government or from Prince Max of Baden, the man who would be his last chancellor, towards the granting of concessions to democracy.

Yet by now, the strain of having to keep her husband's spirits up and years of giving moral support to the man who was in theory if not in practice the most powerful man in Europe were about to prove too much for her. For some time she had been suffering from hear trouble, and during August she suffered a stroke at Wilhelmshöhe which paralysed the left side of her face and her left arm. Thanks to a team of skilled doctors, her condition was quickly stabilised. She was ordered to take a complete rest, confined to bed for several weeks, and placed on a strict diet of cold foods. While he was on a tour of the naval shipyards at Kiel, the Emperor came to visit her. Although both war and Emperor were increasingly unpopular in Germany, the people still had great affection for their Empress, and during an appearance at the Krupp factories in Essen on 18 September, he noticed the evident sympathy that was expressed for her plight and her ill-health.

Shortly afterwards the Emperor had another collapse, similar to that of ten years previously which was construed as a nervous breakdown. His doctors placed him on a similar regimen to that of his wife, and he was ordered to stay away from any business to do with the conduct of the war for several weeks. Although she was still far from well herself, as soon as she was told of his condition, she forced herself out of bed so she could go to his side and spent several days with him, nursing him and restoring his confidence and strength. He was aware that she was putting her own health at risk for her sake, and was coming to respect her more than ever.

Military matters were now going from bad to worse, and there was an increasing mood in Germany that the war was lost. Count Hertling resigned as chancellor on 29 September, and at first it was difficult to find anybody who would take on the poisoned chalice as defeat was evidently looming. Four days later the Emperor's distant cousin Prince Max of Baden, the man who at one time had been considered as a possible husband for his younger sister Margaret and thus become his brother-in-law, was appointed.

The Emperor was now especially punctilious in keeping his wife informed on what was happening, even if the news was bad. General Frederick von Gontard was despatched to inform her in person about the crisis in the Reichstag with the resignation of one chancellor and the appointment of another, Germany's military setbacks, the growing unpopularity of the monarchy, and in short the inevitability of German defeat before long. He found her frail but composed. After he had reported to her and been gracefully dismissed, she sat in her apartment for several hours as she contemplated everything he had told her.

When she summoned her trusted friend, the lady-in-waiting Countess Mathilde Keller, the latter was astonished by her bearing. Though she was desperately sad at their increasingly bleak situation, and at times could do little more than watch helplessly as events took their increasingly inevitable course, her composure was remarkable. Although she had never really liked Tsar Nicholas II and had long nursed an antipathy to Empress Alexandra, she was as horrified as other sovereigns and their consorts across Europe when news from Bolshevik Russia was brought to them of the massacre of the deposed couple, their children and members of the household, at Ekaterinburg in July.

•••••

The Emperor decided to leave Potsdam for his military command at Spa on 29 October. The Empress hated the idea of being parted from her husband at such a time, but she knew as well as he did that if he was to have any chance of restoring order, he would have to be at his military headquarters. When he said goodbye to her, she collapsed into tears. It was the last time she would ever see him as Emperor. That same day the collapse of the German empire began, when sailors from the imperial navy mutinied, taking the two largest ports, Kiel and Wilhelmshaven, after the commanding officers had ordered what they saw as a final mission against Allied naval forces. Sailors took to the streets of Kiel, singing *La Marseillaise*.

Within ten days Hanover, Frankfurt and Munich were also in the hands of the revolutionaries, setting up workers' and soldiers' councils. Public services came to a standstill in Berlin on 7 November, monarchist and rebel forces exchanged cannon fire across the streets, and railway lines were cut in order to prevent the monarchist forces from sending for reinforcements. The Stadschloss in Berlin was flying the revolutionary flag, and the Empress was furious when her brother-in-law Frederick Leopold hoisted the revolutionary banner above his hunting lodge at Glienicke.

From Spa, the Emperor sent his wife a letter dated 7 November, but it never reached Potsdam as the postal stations nearby were in the hands of the revolutionaries. A second letter was written next day, in which he advised her that he was gathering all the troops from the front, to march on Berlin as soon as an armistice had been declared. Their sons would take over the task of defending her in the event of disturbances until he and the troops could come to her aid. If it was no longer safe for her in Potsdam, she would have to go with the children to Königsberg or Rominten if necessary.

Next day, 9 November, the chancellor received pressure from the Allies that to ensure peace, the Emperor would have to renounce the throne. The chancellor knew that his sovereign would almost certainly never step down of his own accord, and he accordingly composed a personal letter advising him that abdication was vital if civil war in Germany was to be avoided. When the Crown Prince joined his father and his chief of staff read him the letter, he was furious. On reflection, he declared with reluctance that he was prepared to abdicate as German Emperor, but he would remain King of Prussia, until he was persuaded that this was impossible.

The Empress was still at the Neue Palais in Potsdam, recovering from her heart attack and longing to be reunited with her husband, alone except for a few faithful retainers. A few days later she was joined by some of the family, including most of her sons, daughters-in-law and grandchildren. The day her husband fled Germany for the Netherlands, she wrote to her daughter, who had taken refuge with her in-laws at their private estate of Gmunden in Austria. Though she was able to assure her that some of the family were by her side and that they were safe, she was increasingly worried about the Emperor, 'so alone in his misfortune and I am not with him to help him bear it, he who was always wanted and done his best for the Fatherland. May God grant that I should be reunited with him once more.'[11]

The Crown Princess was there to be an ever-present source of support. Cecilie recalled her remaining steadfast and upright, refusing to let herself be overwhelmed by events, even though the future looked increasingly bleak for them all. Her last thoughts were for herself, as she was much more concerned about her country, husband and children. 'Only once did I hear her sorrowfully lamenting that now she would have to give up her charitable work at the institutions to which she was so much attached, and her duties as the mother of her people.'[12]

When she was warned that hostile troops were on their way to the palace, she defiantly refused to leave, protesting angrily that to do so would be nothing less than cowardice. Yet she was angered and frightened by the fear of what might happen. Those who were loyal to the monarchy advised that she should remain in Germany as there had been no immediate threats against her life, and she was regarded as far more popular than her husband. She had never forfeited the respect of her husband's subjects, and many hoped that if she stayed where she was, she might serve as a rallying point for the monarchists, or even possibly pave the way for an eventual restoration of the monarchy.

However, when she was asked what she was going to do, she said without hesitation that her place was by that of her husband, and she would join him in exile. She could not bear the thought of being apart from her husband at a time when he needed her more than ever. The newly formed Council of People's Commissars granted her permission to cross the German border into the Netherlands, now that her husband had given his word that he would abdicate. Queen Wilhelmina of the Netherlands was likewise anxious that she should join him, in order to give his stay in her country 'a more private character'. Once she had made the decision to join him, she began to pack as much as she could take with her, gathering up everything from clothes and jewels to cutlery and knickknacks, as she could not face the idea of thieves misappropriating her private possessions.

As the revolution gathered apace and the spectre of events in St Petersburg under the Bolsheviks a year earlier loomed large, with Marxist Communists fighting with the more moderate elements for government control, it became impossible to protect the Neue Palais and those who were still there. There were attempts on the lives of the Emperor's brother Henry and on some of the other princes, and while nobody was harmed, it was enough to make the imperial family realise that they were in danger. Bands of rioters tried to break into the palace, and the detachment of guards sent to defend the Empress were loyal but found it impossible to defend the premises adequately. Eitel Frederick persuaded his mother to come and take refuge nearby in Villa Ingenheim, his home at Potsdam which was thought to be safer from the red menace. She left just in time, for shortly after her departure, crowds broke in, ransacked the ground floor, and helped themselves to antiques, furniture and clothes.

Ingenheim proved to be no less vulnerable and insecure. The guards assigned to protect her proved that they supported the revolution by wearing red cockades, although they too had great respect for their Empress and did what they could to protect her. Yet some held true to their new republican ideals, and on the first night that she was there, a group of drunken sailors broke into the building and overpowered the guards. They went through the rooms to look for her diaries and letters, and when they found her she was interrogated by an officer.

Although she was still very unwell, she faced them bravely and when they suggested that she might like to sit down, she stood defiantly, saying that she was accustomed to sit down only when she felt like it. By sheer force of character she managed to subdue them, and afterwards she was left in peace. The rest of the time at the villa, she remained in total seclusion. She was still suffering from continual heart pain and fatigue, exacerbated by stress, and spent much of her time in bed. The only thing that eased her suffering was the presence of three of her sons, Eitel Frederick, Oscar, Augustus William, and their wives and children, as well as the Crown Princess. Two of her sons were elsewhere, the Crown Prince in Wierigen Island, and Adalbert in Kiel.

On 26 November she completed packing as much as she could, mostly jewels, clothes and personal items. Most of her crown jewels had been spirited away to safety and were in the care of her cousin Queen Victoria of Sweden, daughter of the Dowager Grand Duchess of Baden. Next morning she left Potsdam for the last time. Escorted by soldiers from Eitel Frederick's regiment in civilian clothes to safety outside the German border, and accompanied by a small group including her ever-faithful friend Countess Keller, her dachshund Topsy, and one or two attendants, she left Ingenheim and was driven by the Crown Princess to Charlottenburg Station. There she left Germany in a specially prepared black train, and was provided by the government with an escort from the First Guards

Regiment, to accompany her to the border and then disembark. They did not wear the traditional dress uniform, but instead they were attired in civilian clothes.

The journey through German territory was performed at breakneck speed, in order to ensure that she left the former empire while public opinion was still in her favour. While her companions chatted and passed the time by playing cards, she sat in isolation at the back of the train, attended only by Countess Keller. She would never see her country again.

- 8 -

Exile and death, 1918-21

Now no longer Her Imperial Majesty Empress Augusta, the former first lady of the German Empire joined her husband at Amerongen on 28 November. For them both, it was the sad end of an era, being the day on which he formally signed a document of abdication as German Emperor and King of Prussia. According to one observer, she looked ill and worn as she arrived at the station. Her husband had come to meet her, and was standing alone on the bridge over the moat surrounding their new home. When he looked up to see his wife with whom he was reunited at last, he stood to attention and gave her a military salute. Then with tears in her eyes, she ran over and embraced him, for the first time in public.

Ever since the fall of the German empire, the Empress had been considerably disturbed by threats from the victorious Allied powers to have him brought before the courts as a war criminal. She was sure her husband's life was in danger. Her greatest fear was that he, or maybe even both of them, would be kidnapped, that someone would carry them off to England or France, and that they would ultimately share the fate of Nicholas and Alexandra. Ever since hearing of the fate of both the latter, she had dreaded the possibility that the more vengeful elements among their defeated subjects might be inspired to deal with them in similar fashion. At Christmas she wrote a farewell letter to their children in case they never saw each other again, assuring them that neither of their parents would ever allow themselves to be handed over to the enemy.

By now she was a shadow of her former self, her health undermined if not shattered by the revolution and the toppling of her family from the throne. The newspapers reported with regularity that she was 'dangerously ill', as if not expected to live long. It was inevitable that she would have difficulty in adapting herself to changed circumstances, from consort Empress to exile, in fear for her life and safety and that of her husband and family. Her pride, nourished by being one of the great ladies of the old European order, prevented her from accepting her new fate with placid resignation.

From the day of her arrival in the Netherlands, she kept herself to the small suite of rooms that had been set aside for her to use on the upper floor of the castle. At first the only person admitted into her presence was her long-standing friend and lady-in-waiting Countess Keller. Sombre, morose and severely depressed, at first she refused to take any part in what little court life there was at her new home, and she took her meals alone.

In the spring of 1919 Miss Brenda Tarkington, a young American lady who had been employed by the Empress as a governess to the children, gave an interview to an American journal shortly after having visited her in exile. She said the former first lady of the German empire had aged beyond recognition in last few months. Her features were haggard and careworn, and she lived in terror of her life. The air of stateliness and majesty which had made her such a dignified figure at Court were now gone, and she was 'bent with grief and a broken heart'. She said that she had hoped the Emperor's abdication and his residence in Holland would ease matters in Berlin, but instead things had gone from bad to worse. The darkest stories reached her every day, and 'seldom an hour passes that someone does not bring tidings of a fresh plot'.

Some extraordinary things, she said, had happened to her in recent weeks. One evening towards the end of the first week in February, she was having coffee after dinner, and not feeling very well at the time. After sipping her coffee she realised she could not drink any more because it tasted so peculiar. Just before midnight, she was told that the servant who brought it to her had been taken ill, and she sent her physician to find out further details. After he had administered to the girl, he returned to the Empress and told her the coffee she had been given contained something with a very bitter taste. When he examined it, he found that it had been mixed with several grains of hyoscine, a drug which can cause respiratory failure and death if administered in large doses. He told her that she had had a narrow escape from serious illness at the very least, inferring that there must have been a plot on the part of some of her servants to poison her. In her delicate state of health, it could have been fatal. The police were accordingly sent for, and three of her formerly most trusted maids were arrested for their complicity in the episode. Ever since, she had been very careful not to touch food of any description without the assurance of her physicians that it was perfectly safe for consumption. 'These incidents, of course,' she said, 'point to what I have feared – namely, a conspiracy to kill me, my son, and my only daughter.' She then showed Miss Tarkington copies of unsigned letters she had received, saying, 'Your days are numbered; no power on earth can save you.'

In a subsequent letter to her former governess, the Empress wrote:

> My heart is too full. Too heavy, for me to write to you at any length. Am unutterably miserable at the present time. The most sinister rumours reach me daily, accompanied by anonymous correspondence, containing all kinds of dreadful threats. I had hoped to spend the few remaining years of my life in peace and quiet, but the same hands which put the Tsar Nicholas and his family to death are ready when the opportunity comes to remove me and mine also. My life, indeed, is a horrible nightmare. The awful tidings and warnings which come to me at almost every hour of the day have completely shattered my always poor nervous system. I have not forgotten Russia, and something within me seems to tell me that the ex-Emperor and I are doomed to a like fete. I have had grave news from Holland. The ex-Emperor is in low health and unable to rest or sleep. One does not know what the morrow may bring forth. I am prepared for anything.

When Miss Tarkington met an old friend of the Empress in the train to Berlin on her way back, she said sadly, 'The Empress is fading to a shadow'.[1]

● ● ● ● ●

One of the few activities which the former Empress did pursue with pleasure was writing letters. Most often of all, she wrote to her daughter, who was still living with her in-laws at Gmunden. 'Perhaps I would get some strength back if I had something to do in my own home,' she wrote sadly to her daughter. 'Here, I always have melancholy thoughts and, at the most, letters to write.'[2] Another activity which gave her some pleasure was her knitting, and she had-made several hundred articles of clothing which were to be given to children living in the poorest parts of Germany, for distribution by the Red Cross, of which she had once been the head. Apart from her husband, Countess Keller, who served her all her meals, remained the only other person whom she saw regularly. Besides family and staff, the only people she would receive were children from the nearby village of Zuiderzee, and she was fascinated to see them in their old-fashioned country attire.

Yet the former German Emperor and Empress were still living in luxury, compared to some other royals who had abdicated or been deposed after the war and found themselves having to manage on very little. Nicholas and Alexandra had been reduced to pitiful circumstances for their final months of captivity, and the more recently deposed Charles and Zita of Austria-Hungary were also experiencing some hardship. As well as fifty servants who waited on them, the former sovereigns of Germany had over a hundred courtiers who had joined them in exile, although perhaps not all had done so from strictly honourable motives. Some of them accompanied the former monarchs out of fear of falling into insignificance with the collapse of the monarchy. William and Augusta Victoria were allowed to keep twenty-five train carts sent by the German government full of personal belongings, including furniture, an automobile and a boat. The new republican administration also agreed to acknowledge a number of the Hohenzollerns' privately-owned properties in Berlin that were worth several million. The Emperor had a large sum tied up in stocks and bonds, although these were not liquidated until 1926, and the assets that they brought with them helped them to fund their daily routine in some comfort. Meals were attended by no less than twenty people, the former Emperor and his aides took leisurely afternoon walks in the parks around Amerongen, and courtiers were able to insist on having all their expenses paid.

Even so, comfort was not everything, and the Empress's frame of mind led to deep depression, which she blamed on the 'catastrophe' which had befallen her family. According to one of the hangers-on at their temporary home, she had been much more affected by the overthrow of the Hohenzollerns than her husband. His moods varied between acute depression, bitterness and resignation, possibly tinged with a sense of relief that he was now freed of his burdens and could live like a private citizen, even though his pride might prevent him from admitting as much. Yet in his memoirs, which he had just begun writing and were published in 1922, he acknowledged that 'the revolution broke the Empress's heart.' She aged visibly from the time of their abdication, 'and could not resist her bodily ills with her previous strength. Thus, her decline soon began. The hardest of all for her to bear was her homesickness for Germany, for the German people.'[3]   To their daughter, he wrote that she 'suffers dreadfully and her condition often makes me despair, especially when the pain overcomes her.'[4] More than anything else, she only wanted to return to Potsdam so she could live in complete retirement with her sons and grandsons, but she knew this would always be denied her.

The ex-Crown Prince could see that she was clearly physically ill, 'but will not give way; she knows only one thought, namely, the welfare of my father and of us all, and has only one wish, which is to lighten for us what we have to bear.'[5] The doctor paid her regular visits, but he could do nothing more than to prescribe for her in order to make her more comfortable. Norah Bentinck believed that the Empress considered her husband had been divinely ordained, and 'when the foundations of this her world were scattered she could only think it was because malign forces had triumphed'.[6]

As the former Empress visibly declined, her husband became bitterly resentful, blaming others for his reversal of fortune. He was now very worried, as was his wife, that regular demands by foreign governments for his extradition would be successful, and that he would be put on trial for war crimes. David Lloyd George, who had been appointed British Prime Minister during the war, publicly called for him to be hanged. Some commentators thought he was being rhetorical rather than in deadly earnest, as Britain was in the throes of a general election campaign at the time, and that such soundbites were no more than a crude appeal for votes from the more vengeful elements of his electorate. Nevertheless his rhetoric depressed and worried her still more, as a further series of hammer blows to the peace and mind of an already ageing and sick woman. By March 1920 the Prime Minister had agreed to drop his demands, and he declared that the former ruler was solely the responsibility of the Netherlands.

Queen Wilhelmina had already declared that she and her government would never agree to his extradition, and there the matter ended. It may have been some relief to the Empress, but by then the psychological damage had already been done.

•••••

In August 1919 the former Emperor bought a country house at Doorn, five miles west of the property at Amerongen which had never been intended as more than a temporary measure, and they moved in there on 15 May 1920. While he was making the final arrangements, she took charge of furnishing their new home. For a while, as she threw herself with enthusiasm into the job, she seemed to be almost her old self again. Two months earlier the Duchess of Brunswick had come to visit her parents, a journey made difficult by an outbreak of fighting in the streets of Berlin and Potsdam between monarchists and republicans. Her husband and children had to return quickly to Gmunden for their own safety, and it was with some misgivings that she went on to Amerongen. Delighted as she was to be reunited with her parents, she was deeply upset to see the change in her mother's appearance.[7]

By this time the Empress was too weak to climb the stairs, and a lift had to be installed to allow her to move between floors and save her dwindling energies. Yet the presence of her daughter as well as the joy of finding and placing furniture in Huis Doorn helped to reinvigorate her, as well as giving her the chance to focus on something other than their problems. With her strong belief in the sanctity of marriage, she was also grieved at the collapse of several of the marriages among her sons. The Crown Princess had separated from her unfaithful husband. Eitel Frederick and Lotte, who fortunately had no children, were also shamelessly indulging in extra-marital affairs, and it was evident that their marriage had collapsed although their divorce was not finalised for another five years.

The marriage of Augustus William and Alexandra Victoria was likewise in trouble. They had one son, but what were discreetly known as the prince's 'homophilic tendencies' had exacerbated the problems between them, and they were divorced in March 1920. Joachim and Marie Augusta were also bitterly at odds with each other. The shining exceptions were Adalbert and Adelaide, who had settled down with their two children in Switzerland, and Oscar and Ina, the parents of three children who were also all content with their lot.

The Empress never ceased to dote on her grandchildren, and she always seemed a little brighter when they were with her. The Emperor had grown closer to this fifth son than the others, and was at last ready to forgive him for having made a morganatic marriage. As head of the house of Hohenzollern, even though he was no longer a reigning sovereign, he bestowed upon his daughter the style and title of Her Royal Highness the Princess of Prussia. Even if it was little more than an empty gesture, it was one which pleased the family.

Even as they were moving into Doorn, the Empress was visibly beginning to lose heart, and she undoubtedly knew it would not be her home for long. Heart trouble, arthritis and high blood pressure had made her old and frail beyond her years, and she was confined to a wheelchair for most of the time. The loss of their throne was one thing, but perpetual anxiety over the possible fate of the husband whom she had loved devotedly for all his faults for nearly forty years, and who remained a potential victim of kidnappers although no longer the processes of law, was telling on her even more. Moreover she was grieved to see her children forced into exile, especially at a time when some of their marriages were ending acrimoniously in separation and divorce.

A few days after they had settled in, they were visited by the Crown Prince and Joachim. The Crown Prince had been a regular visitor of theirs, although his movements on Wieringen Island were carefully monitored, and he could only leave the island and come with the permission of the Dutch government. One day when he came to call, he found his parents sitting outside. To help the Empress feel more at home, her husband had had an elaborate rose garden planted near her rooms. The garden at Doorn included a species of rose which had been named in her honour in 1890. Once it was completed, the Emperor had a small greenhouse built so that fresh roses could be grown and delivered daily to her room. Yet the beautiful gardens at the Neue Palais in Potsdam which the Empress had tended for so many years were what she missed most of all about their life in exile. When her eldest son commented to her on the glory which surrounded them, she commented sadly how lovely it was, but alas, it was not 'her' Potsdam, not 'her' home. 'If you only knew how homesickness often gnaws at me within. Oh, I shall never see my home again.'[8]

The Emperor had been increasingly irritated by his sons' undignified behaviour, particularly towards their wives, and with his puritanical streak he disapproved especially of Joachim's heavy gambling. Having always been publicly critical of his late uncle King Edward VII's passion for betting and cards, it was not surprising that he took a firm line with this son who was also falling temptation to the same vice. Joachim had often been a sickly youngster, a factor ascribed to his premature birth, and the Empress was always particularly protective of him, ready to make excuses for his misdemeanours.

Unhappily for them all, the child who had displayed behavioural difficulties had grown up to be a maladjusted, neurotic adult and a bad husband, although the latter could be said equally of most of his brothers. Joachim had bought a villa in Switzerland after the war, but was unable to settle down there. He suffered from depression while he gambled his money away, evidently for want of anything better to do with his time. It was alleged that he beat his wife, who had fled the marital home at least once. He filed for divorce, and won custody of their son. Although the Empress was delighted to see him, the Emperor was furious and ordered him out of the house. Mother and son had a last tearful embrace as they said goodbye, leaving them both in a mood of great gloom.

On 13 July 1920 she had a heart attack and was confined to her bed. The Duke and Duchess of Brunswick arrived later that week, and the doctor warned them that she would have to greet them from her bedchamber. Although he believed that her heart was better, there was an increase in breathlessness, yet he hoped that 'if no unforeseen troubles arise, good progress will be made.'[9]

Meanwhile Joachim had reached the end of the road. He did not return to Switzerland, but instead he visited one of their old homes in Potsdam, Villa Leignitz. On the afternoon of 18 July, three days after his sister arrived at Doorn, he shot himself. He was found by attendants and taken to St Joseph's Hospital nearby, where he died of his wounds a few hours later. When his father was told, there were at least two versions of how he reacted. One said that he collapsed in a chair, utterly shocked, then pulled himself together. Another suggested that he was beside himself with rage that 'the oaf' should have done such a thing to them, and especially to his mother.

He and her physician Dr Haehner solemnly warned the household that the Empress must never be told the truth. She was already in poor health, and they feared that the shock would surely kill her. When he told her that their beloved youngest son had been killed in an accident, she immediately interrupted him.[10] Though she took the news calmly, 'and with the usual composure she exhibited when fate dealt her severe blows,',[11] everyone around them was sure that she knew the truth, and she realised that they were trying to shield her.

Rather irrationally, and ever ready to look for scapegoats, the Emperor maintained that the betrayal of the German people in November 1918 by 'a rabble of Jews' was what had brought about Joachim's death, and was thus responsible for the decline in his wife's condition.[12] Both of them were denied permission to travel to Germany in order to be present at their son's funeral at Potsdam. While three of their sons attended, with Hindenburg and Ludendorff also in attendance, all his mother and father could do was to send a large wreath.

The ex-Crown Prince went to Doorn to be with his mother and comfort her in 'the first and severest hours of her sorrow. What a deal of suffering destiny has heaped upon this poor and sick maternal heart.'[13] According to her sister-in-law Victoria, the widowed Princess Adolf of Schaumburg-Lippe, Joachim's death was the blow that finally broke her spirit.[14]

After Joachim's funeral, the Emperor declared that the childless Eitel Frederick ought to have sole custody of Charles, the dead prince's three-year-old boy, who was often brought to the house for extended visits and stays with his grandparents. About a year later, a German court would rule that the ex-Emperor had no legal authority to issue such an edict, and the little boy was returned to his widowed mother. Yet while he was at Doorn, he brought something approaching an atmosphere of gaiety to what had become a very gloomy residence. Moreover, as a living link with his father, he had a special bond with his grandmother. Yet she was now far too ill to run and play with him, and she was reduced to watching him from her wheelchair as he played in the garden, or sitting with him at lunchtime.

In the autumn he was joined by his elder cousins, the children of the former Crown Prince. The Emperor and Empress loved entertaining all their grandchildren, and the former felt invigorated as he heard them laughing while they played together in the halls or the garden.

The ex-Crown Princess came to visit her mother-in-law in August 1920, and was shocked to find her looking so delicate and frail. Yet the latter was as kind and affectionate as ever, and the younger woman thought that 'she had grown perhaps even more tender-hearted in her foreign environment'. Even so, it was obvious that she was suffering immeasurably from having been cut off from her own country. When Cecile took her leave of the Empress and looked at her in the doorway of the house, 'my heart told me that I would never see this devoted mother here on earth again'.[15]

On 22 October they all gathered to celebrate the Empress's sixty-second birthday, yet it was a mournful occasion. She spent the day in bed, from which she had hardly been able to move for several days. The Crown Prince sat beside her while she held his hand, listening to him telling her 'a number of amusing and harmless little anecdotes' concerning his household, as he watched her features light up every now and again with just a flicker of former times . On the rare occasions that she was strong enough to get up, she would walk slowly and painfully through the rooms as 'her tired eyes' wandered caressingly over all the old furniture and memories that had come from Berlin and Potsdam. To her family, it seemed 'as though she were bidding them all a silent farewell'.[16]

Everyone recognised that she was not long for this world. She suffered several heart attacks, complicated by the formation of blood clots, and by the end of November she was generally only semi-conscious during the day. A member of the household told reporters, who had been warned to expect her death at any time, that she fully realised the seriousness of her condition, was quite resigned, and actually longed for the end of her sufferings.[17]

Still she was not to be allowed the peace of mind for which she craved. She had convinced herself that there would be no end to the plots and attempts to kidnap, even murder her and her husband. Obsessed by and fearful for their personal safety, she slept very badly at night because every little noise woke her, and she was terrified that somebody had come to carry out the threats. Almost every night she would scream that 'they' were coming for them, and then burst into tears. The previous year a group of American officers based in Luxembourg had attempted to break into Amerongen but were foiled. Nevertheless, the Emperor was not going to take chances, and he installed a police guard to protect them.

At Christmas 1920 she was surrounded by her children and grandchildren, as she had requested, but she made few appearances during the festivities. By now she could no longer even leave her wheelchair to walk a few steps unaided, but spent her days in bed, rarely sleeping, only semi-conscious much of the time. The children often used to come and sit at her bedside at night. One night when Augustus William was watching over her, she bade all of the children goodbye in her sleep.

On 22 January 1921 her brother Ernst Gunther, five years her junior, passed away. As she was now so frail, the news was kept from her. By the time of her fortieth wedding anniversary she was only conscious for a few hours each day. According to her eldest son, the anniversary was no cause for celebration. Everything in the house, he remarked, 'was sad and depressed', with his mother confined to her couch, so feeble that she could hardly speak. As they were warned that the end could not be far off, in March her five sons came back to Doorn, but unrest in Germany in Austria delayed their sister's arrival. The princes maintained a constant vigil between them. Silence reigned most of the time, as even simple conversation exhausted her. On the days when she felt a little stronger, she was propped up against her pillows next to the window where she could look out at the spring flowers, while Dr Haehner relieved her pain with frequent hypodermic injections.

According to the British Legation at The Hague, she had been sinking for some time. Several times, a representative said, she had been 'apparently dead but has been restored to life by the skill of her physician and the use of saline injections'.[18] Having nothing left to live for, she would probably not have thanked them.

Shortly after midnight on 11 April there was a change in her breathing for the worse. The doctor and Countess Keller and the nurse gently moved her into a position which they hoped would make her more comfortable as her pulse gradually weakened. Her husband and Prince Adalbert were summoned to her bedside, and at about 5.30 a.m. she slipped away.

● ● ● ● ●

Tributes to her from far and wide came to Doorn. Amongst their subjects there may have been very little enthusiasm for her husband as Emperor, but she had always been regarded with the utmost respect, and the mourning was widespread. It pained the Emperor that no message of condolence was forthcoming from King George V or the British royal family. Nevertheless the rest of the family, many of whom had had their differences with her in the past, were full of praise as they paid tributes to her memory. Her sister-in-law Victoria, now living in her late husband's ancestral home at Bonn, spoke for them all when she wrote some six years or so later in her memoirs that she had been 'a model wife and mother', who had set an example to her country which was admired by all and followed by many. 'During the trying years of the war she had always been the first to sacrifice herself to her country and to encourage others to do so.'[19]

In London, the judgment on the hapless wife of the fallen enemy was suitably and admirably objective. The writer of her obituary in *The Times* observed with some compassion that

> The war seems finally to have hardened her. It was the culmination of an existence in which she had been little else but a lay figure. She believed as a matter of principle in the triumph of German arms, but there is no evidence that she had formed any conception of what was at stake. Whatever her

emotions may have been she controlled them, but in the discharge of her public functions she grew year by year less spontaneous.[20]

Her body lay at Doorn with a round-the-clock vigil presided over by her husband and sons, all attired in full military uniform. Throughout the room there were pine-scented wreaths and bundles of flowers, sent from various members of the family. The ex-Crown Prince spent the first night after her death seated next to her coffin. Stricken with grief, he seemed to have problems in coming to terms with the passing of his mother, and when he came to write and publish his memoirs, he wrote that he seemed unable to grasp the idea that she would be there to speak to him no more, and that her eyes would never again be turned towards him. 'She was the magnet which attracted us children, wherever we might be, toward the parental home. She knew all our wishes, our hopes, our cares. Now she had been taken from us forever.'[21]

Homesick to the last, she had left a wish that she should be buried at Potsdam, where she had known her greatest happiness; as she had told her daughter not long before she passed away, 'I will sleep in my own homeland'.[22] The British Foreign Office was reluctant to endorse such a move, fearing that it would lead to political demonstrations of an embarrassing character. However the republican government agreed to let her be interred in the royal mausoleum at the Neue Palais at Potsdam; but with the stipulation that to avoid any monarchist sentiments, the train which carried the coffin and its caretakers was required to travel without any fanfare or official ceremonies at any point on German soil until it reached Potsdam.

The German government took great pains to keep many of the details of the funeral a secret in the hop of attracting as little attention as possible. The publicly announced date for the funeral was changed without warning for such a reason. Moreover, her widower was not allowed to attend the funeral or accompany her coffin any further than the Dutch-German frontier. It was exceptionally painful for him as it meant that he would never be able to stand at his wife's grave, and to his sons would fall the duty of escorting her to her final resting place. Augustus Wilhelm and Eitel Frederick immediately left for Germany to begin making the funeral preparations, while Oscar and Adalbert decided they would accompany the coffin on its last journey.

Instead of having a funeral at Doorn, the family decided they would hold a small memorial service for her at the train station at Maarn, five miles away. On the night of 17 April her coffin, decorated in the traditional Prussian style with pine fronds, and covered with the standard of the Queen of Prussia, was taken to the station in a specially modified car. Mourners stood along the whole route, their heads bared and bowed low in respect. The only sound that could be heard was the clattering of hooves from the horses pulling the coffin. Behind was a procession of black cars, the first filled with bouquets and funeral wreaths, the second containing Ernest von Dryander, the court chaplain, in his black clerical robes, the third members of the former imperial court.

About ten minutes after these vehicles arrived at Maarn a fourth vehicle filled up, and Oscar and Adalbert stepped out, both in the uniform of the Prussian Guards, with black spiked helmets and grey capes over their shoulders, while ex-Crown Prince William was attired in the uniform of a general of the Brandenburg Infantry. The Duchess of Brunswick and the other women wore black mourning, in contrast to the military uniforms being worn by the men. As well as her widower and children, the service was attended by former courtiers, government officials, and representatives sent on behalf of Queen Wilhelmina, King Alfonso XIII of Spain, and King Gustav V of Sweden.

As the simple ceremony began, Dr Dryander gathered everybody on the station platform around the coffin, where he said a few emotional words. Reporters noticed that the Emperor wept bitterly throughout as he stood over his wife's coffin. After the short service, Adalbert, Oscar and the other male members of the court loaded their mother's casket into the last of three dark green compartments attached to the funeral train, which was scheduled to leave before dawn the next morning. Sleeping on the train that night were the two princes, Dr Dryander, and the Empress's ladies-in-waiting, who had arranged to return to Germany after the funeral. In the morning they would accompany the coffin back to Potsdam. The Crown Prince asked the Dutch government for permission to return as well but he was told that if he did, he would not be allowed to return to the Netherlands.

Accompanied by the Duchess of Brunswick, father and son boarded the train for a final farewell to the woman they had both loved. Then the Emperor went into the travel car to thank those who were sleeping on board for their devotion to the Empress in accompanying her body to Potsdam. When he came out a few minutes later, according to an American reporter present, he looked like 'a man broken by sorrow'.[23] Without a further word, he and his daughter got back into the car and were driven back to Doorn. The Duke of Brunswick and the ex-Crown Prince and the rest of the courtiers who were staying in Holland followed them soon afterwards.

The funeral train left Maarn at 7.45 a.m. Plans had been made for William to return and see the train leave Dutch soil, but he had reportedly suffered badly that night from 'severe nervous depression', and could not bring himself to return to the station at the moment of departure. The Dutch government paid their respects by flying their flags at half-mast at every station through which the train passed on its way to Germany while several thousand citizens, who had never seen the Empress, lined the tracks. At about 10.00 a.m. the train crossed the border into Germany, and from that moment the route was lined by crowds in their thousands, mostly dressed in mourning, and many kneeling in prayer. Church bells sounded across the republic, and the British representative in Berlin estimated in a report to the Foreign Office that about 200,000 people visited Potsdam for the occasion.

Despite what the republican government may have felt, there was evidently a huge feeling of affection and respect for the late Empress, as indicated by all the mourners who had turned out to witness her final journey home. The journey from Maarn to Potsdam, a distance of nearly four hundred miles, was lined in an unbroken human chain of about ten thousand mourners, all echoing 'The Empress is coming!' So many people were there that the train was forced to delay its arrival in Potsdam. Several towns forced the convoy to stop at their stations so that their citizens would have a chance to mourn. Thousands of people, all dressed in black, fell to their knees and prayed. In some towns church bells rang, choirs sang, and bands played hymns. The Duchess of Brunswick was comforted to observe how people were all 'mourning their beloved Empress'.[24]

On 19 April the train pulled into Wildpark Station near Potsdam before dawn. The funeral took place later that day. By the time the coffin reached Potsdam, it was covered in wreaths laid by people who had lined the route. When the passengers disembarked, they were met by Eitel Frederick, Augustus William, Adalbert and Oscar, ex-Crown Princess Cecilie, alongside several other royals and former imperial officials, as Dr Dryander recited prayers as each person came to pay his or her personal respects. When the ceremony was over, the two military regiments that had been her personal units, the Pasewalker Cuirassiers and the 86th Schleswig-Holstein Infantry, formed a guard of honour and stood watch over the coffin for the rest of the night.

The funeral cortege was surrounded by hundreds of people in the procession from the station to her final resting place, the Antique Temple, a great domed mausoleum which had been built by Frederick the Great at Sans-Souci Park. Acting as pallbearers were four knights of the Order of the Black Eagle, the highest order of Prussian chivalry. Apart from the Empress Frederick, she was the only woman who had ever been a recipient of the Order. Immediately behind them followed her sons Oscar, Eitel Frederick, Adalbert and Augustus William, with her daughters-in-law Ina and Adelaide, all heads bowed low. An estimated 200,000 spectators or more were there, all standing in respectful silence as the procession moved through the streets. There was a remarkable lack of noise, and likewise no pushing or shoving, as they all came to say their last farewell.

After the coffin had been placed in front of the altar in the mausoleum, the princes took over the vigil, their swords drawn, as Dr Dryander gave the funeral oration, praising the former Empress as mother and woman, 'one who placed duty above everything else.'[25] To conclude the funeral, the pastor read an excerpt from the gospels, after which the casket was placed in the Antique Temple, next to where the body of her son Joachim had been laid to rest less than a year before.

That same day, her widower commented with bitterness in a letter to Irma von Fürstenberg about his exclusion from Germany. 'What every common worker can do, namely follow his wife's coffin to the grave, even that has been made impossible for me by my traitorous people!'[26]

The man who had been left behind, denied a chance to pay his last respects in person, had long been preparing himself for the worst, but even so, he was stricken with grief. When the Duchess of Brunswick arrived to help nurse him through an attack of bronchitis soon afterwards, she found him looking 'timid and embarrassed, and I believe he did not wish the world to see the dreadful despair which had overcome him.'[27] He turned his wife's bedroom into a shrine devoted to her memory, with a cross of flowers draped across her bed. Once a week, for the rest of his twenty years, he would retire there on his own, to go and mourn her memory.

In his memoirs, published the following year, covering the years from 1878 to 1918, he devoted one short heartfelt paragraph in the final chapter to his wife of thirty years. At that stage, perhaps he felt unable to write any more:

> The revolution broke the Empress's heart. She aged visibly from November, 1918, onward, and could not resist her bodily ills with her previous strength. Thus, her decline soon began. The hardest of all for her to bear was her homesickness for Germany, for the German people. Notwithstanding this, she still tried to afford consolation for me.[28]

When he came to write *My Early Life*, a second volume of memoirs four years later, covering his life from birth to accession to the throne, she was mentioned many more times. After he had described her family, their first meetings, betrothal and wedding, he referred warmly to their happy domestic life, 'surrounded as we were by many fine, thriving children'. He also paid a graceful tribute to the woman who was his companion and the mother of his people, who in the end sacrificed her life for his sake. 'My thoughts are often at that grave in German soil, on which I am forbidden even to lay a flower.'[29]

Not long before her death, Empress Augusta Victoria had told her husband that he must marry again. Within less than two years he had taken her at her word. In November 1922, the former Emperor found a second wife in a widow who was some twenty-eight years his junior, Her Serene Highness Hermine, Princess of Reuss. They were fifth cousins, sharing a common descent from George II of Great Britain. His brother Henry, sisters Victoria and Margaret attended the ceremony, as did his two eldest sons, ex-Crown Prince William and Eitel Frederick, but the other three princes and his daughter did not approve, and were all conspicuous by their absence.

The marriage endured, although Dr Haehner was convinced that her sole motive for marrying him lay in her expectation that the German monarchy would be restored and one day she would wear the crown of an Empress. He was sure that it would all fall apart once she saw her hopes and dreams were in vain, and that 'the game [was] absolutely up for her.'[30] It never did, but if she had ever nursed some ambitions as an Empress Consort, it was no foundation for a happy union. When the Duchess of Brunswick visited her father at Doorn a year later, she was shocked to see what a state her father was in, and at how critical he and his second wife had become

107

of each other. Other observers would later comment that husband and wife did not seem particularly content together, with each one grumbling about the other.

William died in June 1941, aged eighty-two, less than two years after the outbreak of the Second World War. After his death Hermine returned to Germany, where she died in 1947, aged fifty-nine.

●●●●●

Augusta Victoria was the third German Empress as well as the last. The first, her grandmother-in-law Augusta of Saxe-Weimar, the consort of Emperor William I, had not played a particularly active role, partly because of indifferent health and partly because her political views, intellectual and artistic gifts had conspicuously not been appreciated by the soldier husband with whom she had never had anything in common, or his entourage. Victoria, born Princess Royal of Great Britain, the most gifted and remarkable personality of the three, had been first lady of the land for a mere three tragic months while her husband was dying, although before and after his reign she had worked unceasingly as much as her health permitted on behalf of her charities, artistic and educational institutions. For much of her thirty years as Empress her daughter-in-law had generally been content to remain in the background, devoting herself to the traditional German roles of *Kirche, Küche, Kinder*. It was only after the crises of 1908 and the temporary mental collapse of her husband that she began to play a more prominent role in supporting him out of necessity.

Some of her contemporaries found her aloof, arrogant, bigoted, xenophobic, or just plain boring. Moreover, she certainly never mastered the art of making friends with the other European royalties with whom she came into contact. Married to such a mercurial man whose mental stability was questionable at the best of times, a ruler and figurehead who would come to be hated and despised throughout Europe, she was faced with a difficult task which she managed to the best of her ability. But by the time war broke out in 1914, her good qualities had long since been recognised by the German people.

For all her personal faults and shortcomings, she had been a much-loved and respected consort, and for the last few years of their reign as Emperor and Empress it was apparent that she was much more popular than her husband. The mourning throughout the new republic of Germany which followed her death demonstrated that her life had by no means been a failure, and that many of her husband's subjects as well as her sorrowing family never ceased to revere her memory as much, if not more than, the husband whom she had left behind.

Frederick, Duke of Schleswig-Holstein-Sonderburg-Augustenburg

Adelaide, Duchess of Schleswig-Holstein-Sonderburg-Augustenburg

Prince and Princess William of Prussia and their eldest son Prince William

Princess Caroline Matilda, later Duchess of Schleswig-Holstein

Princess Louise Sophie, later Princess Frederick Leopold of Prussia

*Ernst Gunther, Duke of Schleswig-Holstein, and his wife,
formerly Princess Dorothea of Saxe-Coburg Gotha*

The Emperor's sisters, Princesses Margaret, Victoria and Sophie, 1888

Empress Augusta Victoria, about 1892

Emperor William II and Empress Augusta Victoria

Emperor William II and Empress Augusta Victoria, in more
informal dress

The Empress Frederick and Queen Victoria, 1889

Empress Augusta Victoria and her sons

*The state visit to Windsor Castle, November 1907. Front row, l to r, Queen
Maud of Norway; Empress Augusta Victoria; Queen Marie Amelie of
Portugal; Queen Victoria Eugenie of Spain. Back row, l to r, King Alfonso
XIII of Spain; Emperor William II; Queen Alexandra, and King Edward VII
of Great Britain*

Emperor William II, with Crown Prince William and his eldest son,
Prince William, c.1908

Cecilie, Crown Princess

Prince Eitel Frederick and Duchess Sophie Charlotte

Princes Augustus William and Oscar

Prince Adalbert and Princess Adelaide

Empress Augusta Victoria and her daughter Princess Victoria Louise

Empress Augusta Victoria and Queen Mary of England

Prince Bernhard von Bülow, imperial German chancellor, 1900-09

Empress Augusta Victoria , c.1913

Prince Joachim of Germany

*Empress Augusta Victoria and Princess Victoria Louise, later Duchess
of Brunswick*

Empress Augusta Victoria and her grandson Prince Charles,
son of Prince Joachim, c.1920

A view of part of Empress Augusta Victoria's funeral procession, April 1921

The Children of
Empress Augusta Victoria
and Emperor William II

Crown Prince William (1882-1951), 1905 married Duchess Cecilie of Mecklenburg-Schwerin (1886-1954), four sons (one killed in World War II), two daughters. Separated but never formally divorced

Eitel Frederick (1883-1942), 1906 married Duchess Sophie Charlotte of Oldenburg (1879-1964), no children. Divorced 1926

Adalbert (1884-1948), 1914 married Princess Adelaide of Saxe-Meiningen (1891-1971), one son, one daughter (and one stillborn daughter)

Augustus William (1887-1949), 1908 married Princess Alexandra Victoria of Schleswig-Holstein-Sonderburg-Glücksburg (1887–1957), one son. Divorced 1920

Oscar (1888-1958), 1914 married Countess Ina Marie von Bassewitz, created Countess von Ruppin (1888-1973), three sons (one killed in World War II), one daughter

Joachim (1890-1920), 1916 married Princess Marie-Augusta of Anhalt (1898-1983), one son. Divorced 1920

Victoria Louise (1892-1980), 1913 married Ernest Augustus, Duke of Brunswick (1887–1953), four sons, one daughter

Reference Notes

CPFW – Crown Princess Frederick William
EAV – Empress Augusta Victoria
QV – Queen Victoria

Chapter 1

1 Victoria, Queen, *Your Dear Letter*, 205, CPFW to QV, 19.8.1868
2 Röhl I, 330, CPFW to Prince William, 7.5.1878
3 Cecil I, 48; Bülow, 1897-1903, 259
4 Röhl I, 331, CPFW to Princess Christian of Schleswig-Holstein, 8.6.1878
5 ibid, Diary of Crown Prince Frederick William, 30.8.1878
6 ibid, 333, Crown Prince Frederick William to CPFW, 23.9.1878
7 ibid, 337
8 Cecil I, 49
9 Victoria, Queen, *Beloved Mama*, 50, CPFW to QV, 10.7.1879
10 Röhl I, 349
11 Victoria, Queen, *Beloved Mama*, 62, CPFW to QV, 18.1.1880
12 Röhl I, 413
13 ibid, 357
14 Victoria, Queen, *Beloved Mama*, 64, CPFW to QV, 13.2.1880
15 William II, *Gone Astray*, 92-3, 1.6.1880
16 Victoria, *Letters of the Empress Frederick*, 179, CPFW to QV, 26.3.1880
17 Röhl I, 362
18 ibid, 361
19 Cecil I, 52
20 Vovk, 37

Chapter 2

1 Victoria, Queen, *Beloved Mama*, 96, 28.2.1881
2 William II, *Gone Astray,* 94, 27.2.1881
3 Röhl I, 467
4 ibid, 94, 6.5.1882
5 Alice, 92

6 Cecil II, 4

7 Brook-Shepherd, 93

8 Bülow, 1897-1903, 15-6

9 Röhl I, Crown Prince Frederick William to CPFW, 12.11.1883

10 Daisy, *What I left unsaid*, 195

11 Marie of Roumania I, 221

12 Stephanie, 194

13 Poore, 37

14 Corti, *English Empress,* 226, QV to CPFW, 10.1.1885

15 Fischer, 179

16 Pakula, 536

17 Daisy, *What I left unsaid*, 288

18 Röhl I, 454

19 ibid, 675

20 *Letters of the Empress Frederick*, 293, CPFW to QV, 16.3.1888

Chapter 3

1 Victoria, Queen, *Advice to a grand-daughter*, 144, QV to Princess Louis of
   Battenberg, 4.7.1888

2 Fischer, 344

3 Pakula, 536, Empress Frederick to QV, 22.3.1890

4 ibid, 536; Röhl II, 625, Empress Frederick to QV, 16.12.1890

5 Miller, 'The very amiables...' Princess Henry to QV, 19.3.1890

6 Röhl II, 129, EAV to Emperor William II, 23.9.1890

7 Corti, *English Empress,* 337-8

8 *Empress Frederick writes to Sophie,* 76

9 Rohl II, 625, Empress Frederick to QV, 20.1.1891

10 *Empress Frederick writes to Sophie,* 86

11 Corti, *English Empress,* 339, Emperor William II to QV, 13.5.1891

12 Mallet, 52, 21.4.1891

13 Röhl III, 622

14 Alice, 93

15 Cecilie, 211

16 Howard, 149

17 William II, *Memoirs,* 52-3

18 Fischer, 311

19 Röhl II, 626

20 Cecil II, 6

21 William, Crown Prince, *Memoirs*, 14

22 Victoria, *Kaiser's Daughter*, 19

23 Frederick Leopold, 114

24 ibid, 31

25 Bülow, 1897-1903, 258

26 Marie, Queen of Roumania, II, 222

27 Vovk 297, EAV to Prince Chlodwig of Hohenlohe-Schillingsfürst, 29.7.1896

28 *Empress Frederick writes to Sophie,* 96

29 Frederick Leopold, 31

30 Alice, 92

Chapter 4

1 Maylunas & Mironenko, 164-5, Tsar Nicholas II to Empress Marie, 1.8.1897

2 Fischer, 317

3 Röhl II, 626, August Eulenburg to Philipp Eulenburg, 27.12.1897

4 Bülow, 1897-1903, 222

5 Röhl II, 627 Philipp Eulenburg to Bülow, 20.7.1898

6 ibid, 871

7 Pope-Hennessy, 185

8 Bülow, 1897-1903, 288

9, 10 Bülow, 1897-1903, 301

11 Röhl, *Kaiser and Court,* 95

12 Hull, 19

13 Röhl II, 455

14 Bülow, 1897-1903, 455

15 Röhl II, 627

16 Bülow, 1897-1903, 498

17 ibid, 499

18 Röhl II, 628, Philipp Eulenburg to Bülow, 1.10.1901

Chapter 5

1 Schwering, 55

2 Victoria, *Kaiser's Daughter,* 2

3 Fischer, 317-9

4 Daisy, *Diaries,* 70

5 Bülow, 1903-09, 246-7

6 Jonas, 6-7

7 Cecilie, 207-8

8 Marie, Queen of Roumania, II, 228

9 Röhl III, 524, Emperor William II to Frederick, Grand Duke of Baden, 5.3.1906

10 ibid, 524

Chapter 6

1 Bülow, 1903-09, 365
2 ibid, 374
3 ibid, 518
4 Röhl III, 747
5 Cecil II, 7
6 Röhl III, 809
7 ibid, 862
8 Victoria, *Kaiser's Daughter*, 74
9 Topham, 275
10 Anon, *Recollections of three Kaisers*, 308-9

Chapter 7

1 Röhl III, 1085
2 Lamar II, 209
3 Röhl III, 1112, EAV to Emperor William II, 12.8.1914
4 Lutz I, 21-2
5 Victoria of Prussia, 206-7
6 Davis, 167
7 Cecil II, 215
8 Röhl III, 1132
9 ibid, 1168
10 ibid, 1174
11 Victoria, *Kaiser's Daughter,* 144, EAV to Duchess of Brunswick,
    11.11.1918
12 Cecilie, 251

Chapter 8

1 *The Times,* 27.5.1919
2 Victoria, *Kaiser's Daughter,* 148
3 William, Crown Prince, *Memoirs*, 330
4 Victoria, *Kaiser's Daughter,* 147
5 William, Crown Prince, *Memoirs*, 107
6 Bentinck, 35-6
7 Victoria, *Kaiser's Daughter,* 148
8 William, Crown Prince, *Memoirs*, 231
9 Victoria, *Kaiser's Daughter,* 149

10 Röhl III, 1204

11 Victoria, *Kaiser's Daughter,* 150

12 Cecil II, 302

13 William, Crown Prince, *Memoirs,* 184

14 Victoria of Prussia, *Memoirs,* 206

15 Cecilie, 253-4

16 William, Crown Prince, *Memoirs,* 209

17 *New York Times,* 1.12.1920

18 Zeepvat, 'Kirche, Küche, Kinder...'

19 William II, *Memoirs,* 206

20 *The Times,* 12.4.1921

21 William, Crown Prince, *Memoirs,* 281

22 Victoria, *Kaiser's Daughter,* 151

23 *New York Times,* 18.4.1921

24 Victoria, *Kaiser's Daughter,* 151-2

25 *New York Times,* 19.4.1921

26 Röhl III, 1205, ex-Emperor William II to Irma von Fürstenburg, 19.4.1921

27 Victoria, *Kaiser's Daughter,* 150

28 William II, *Memoirs,* 330

29 William II, *My Early Life,* 184

30 Röhl III, 1211-2

Bibliography

Books

The place of publication is London unless otherwise stated

Alice, Countess of Athlone, *For my grandchildren: Some reminiscences*, Evans Bros, 1966

Anon., *Recollections of three Kaisers*, Herbert Jenkins, 1929

Balfour, Michael, *The Kaiser and his times: with an afterword*, Penguin, 1975

Bennett, Daphne, *Vicky, Princess Royal of England and German Empress*, Collins Harvill, 1971

Benson, E.F., *The Kaiser and English relations*, Longmans, Green, 1936

Bentinck, Norah, *The ex-Kaiser in exile*, New York, Doran, n.d.

Brook-Shepherd, Gordon, *Royal sunset: The dynasties of Europe and the Great War*, Weidenfeld & Nicolson, 1987

Bülow, Prince Bernhard von, *Memoirs*, 4 vols., Putnam, 1931

Cecil, Lamar, *Wilhelm II, Vol. 1: Prince and Emperor, 1859-1900*, Chapel Hill, University of North Carolina, 1989

-- *Wilhelm II, Vol. 2: Emperor and Exile, 1900-1941*, Chapel Hill, University of North Carolina, 1996

Cecilie, Crown Princess, *Memoirs*, Victor Gollancz, 1931

Corti, Egon Caesar Conte, *The downfall of three dynasties*, Cassell, 1934

-- *The English Empress: A study in the relations between Queen Victoria and her eldest Daughter, Empress Frederick of Germany*, Cassell, 1957

Daisy, Princess of Pless, *The private diaries, 1873-1914*, John Murray, 1950

-- *What I left unsaid*, Cassell, 1936

Davis, Arthur, *The Kaiser as I knew him*, New York, Harper Bros, 1918

Fischer, Henry W., *The private lives of William II & his Consort: A secret history of the court of Berlin,* Heinemann, 1904

Fontenoy, Mme La Marquise de (Marguerite Cunliffe-Owen), *The Secret Memoirs of the Courts of Europe: William II, Germany; Francis Joseph, Austria-Hungary,* Philadelphia, Barrie, 1900 [accessed online]

Frederick Leopold of Prussia, Princess, *Behind the scenes at the Prussian court,* John Murray, 1939

Howard, Ethel, *Potsdam Princes,* Methuen, 1916

Hull, Isabel V., *The entourage of Kaiser Wilhelm II 1888-1918,* Cambridge University Press, 1982

Jonas, Klaus, *The life of Crown Prince William,* Routledge & Kegan Paul, 1961

Kohut, Thomas August, *Wilhelm II and the Germans: A study in leadership,* New York: Oxford University Press, 1991

Ludwig, Emil, *Kaiser Wilhelm II,* Putnam, 1926

Lutz, Ralph Haswell (ed.), *The fall of the German Empire, 1914-1918,* 2 vols. Stanford: Stanford University Press, 1932

Mallet, Victor, ed. *Life with Queen Victoria: Marie Mallet's letters from Court 1887-1901,* John Murray, 1968

Marie, Duchess of Edinburgh, *Dearest Missy: The correspondence between Marie, Grand Duchess of Russia, Duchess of Edinburgh and of Saxe-Coburg and Gotha and her daughter Marie, Crown Princess of Roumania, 1879-1900,* ed. Diana Mandache, Falkoping, Rosvall, 2011

Marie, Queen of Roumania, *The story of my life,* 3 vols, Cassell, 1934-5

Marie Louise, Princess, *My memories of six reigns,* Evans Bros, 1956

Maylunas, Andrei, & Mironenko, Sergei, *A lifelong passion: Nicolas and Alexandra: Their own story,* Weidenfeld & Nicolson, 1996

Packard, Jerrold, *Victoria's daughters,* New York: St Martin's Press, 1998; Stroud: Sutton, 1999

Pakula, Hannah, *An uncommon woman: The Empress Frederick,* Weidenfeld & Nicolson, 1996

Ponsonby, Sir Frederick, *Recollections of three reigns,* Eyre & Spottiswoode, 1951

Poore, Judith, *The Memoirs of Emily Loch: Discretion in waiting,* Kinloss, Librario, 2007

Pope-Hennessy, James, *Queen Mary, 1867-1953,* Allen & Unwin, 1959

Ridley, Jane, *Bertie: A life of Edward VII*, Chatto & Windus, 2012

Röhl, John, *The Kaiser and his Court: Wilhelm II and the Government of Germany*, Cambridge University Press, 1996

-- *Wilhelm II: The Kaiser's personal monarchy, 1888-1900*, Cambridge University Press, 2004

-- *Wilhelm II: Into the abyss of war and exile, 1900-1941*, Cambridge University Press, 2014

-- *Young Wilhelm: The Kaiser's early life, 1859-1888*, Cambridge University Press, 1998

Rose, Kenneth, *King George V*, Weidenfeld & Nicolson, 1983

Schwering, Count Axel von, *The Berlin Court under William II*, Cassell, 1915

Stephanie of Belgium, Princess, *I was to be Empress*, Ivor Nicholson & Watson, 1937

Topham, Anne, *A distant thunder*, New York, New Chapter Press, 1992

Van der Kiste, John, *Crowns in a changing world: The British and European monarchies 1901-36*, Stroud, Sutton, 1993

-- *Dearest Vicky, Darling Fritz: Queen Victoria's eldest daughter and the German Emperor*, Stroud: Sutton, 2001

-- *Kaiser Wilhelm II: Germany's last Emperor*, Stroud, Sutton, 1999

-- *Kings of the Hellenes: The Greek Kings 1863-1974*, Stroud, Sutton, 1994

-- *Prince Henry of Prussia, 1862-1929*, South Brent, A & F/ CreateSpace, 2015

-- *The Prussian Princesses: Sisters of Kaiser Wilhelm II*, Stroud, Fonthill, 2014

Victoria, Consort of Frederick III, German Emperor, *The Empress Frederick writes to Sophie*, Faber, 1955

-- *Letters of the Empress Frederick*, ed. Sir Frederick Ponsonby, Macmillan, 1928

Victoria, Princess, *The Kaiser's daughter*, W.H. Allen, 1977

Victoria, Queen, *The Letters of Queen Victoria: a Selection from Her Majesty's Correspondence between the years 1837 and 1861*, ed. A.C. Benson & Viscount Esher, 3 vols, John Murray, 1907

-- *The Letters of Queen Victoria, 2nd Series: a Selection from Her Majesty's Correspondence and Journal between the years 1862 and 1885*, ed. G. E. Buckle, 3 vols, John Murray, 1926-8

-- *The Letters of Queen Victoria, 3rd Series: a Selection from Her Majesty's Correspondence and Journal between the years 1886 and 1901,* ed. G.E. Buckle, 3 vols, John Murray, 1930-2

-- *Further Letters of Queen Victoria, from the Archives of the House of Brandenburg-Prussia;* ed. Hector Bolitho, Thornton Butterworth, 1938

-- *Dearest Mama: Private Correspondence of Queen Victoria and the Crown Princess of Prussia, 1861-1864;* ed. Roger Fulford, Evans Bros, 1968

-- *Your Dear Letter: Private Correspondence of Queen Victoria and the Crown Princess of Prussia, 1865-1871,* ed. Roger Fulford, Evans Bros, 1971

-- *Darling Child: Private Correspondence of Queen Victoria and the Crown Princess of Prussia, 1871-1878;* ed. Roger Fulford, Evans Bros, 1976

-- *Beloved Mama: Private Correspondence of Queen Victoria and the German Crown Princess of Prussia, 1878-1885;* ed. Roger Fulford, Evans Bros, 1981

-- *Beloved and Darling Child: Last letters Queen Victoria and her eldest daughter, 1886-1901;* ed. Agatha Ramm, Stroud, Sutton, 1990

-- *Advice to a grand-daughter: Letters from Queen Victoria to Princess Victoria of Hesse,* ed. Richard Hough, Heinemann, 1975

Victoria of Prussia, Princess, *My memoirs,* Eveleigh, Nash & Grayson, 1929; Royalty Digest, 1995

Victoria Louise, Duchess of Brunswick, *The Kaiser's daughter,* ed. Robert Vacha, W.H. Allen, 1977

Vovk, Justin C., *Imperial requiem: Four royal women and the fall of the age of empire,* Bloomington, iUniverse, 2012

Whittle, Tyler, *The last Kaiser: A biography of William II, German Emperor and King of Prussia,* Heinemann, 1977

William II, *Gone Astray: Some leaves from an Emperor's diary,* New York: John Lane, 1918

-- *My Early Life,* Methuen, 1926

-- *My Memoirs: 1878-1918,* Cassell, 1922

William, Crown Prince, *The memoirs of the Crown Prince of Germany,* Thornton Butterworth, 1922

Journals

New York Times

Royalty Digest
The Times

Articles

Eilers Koenig, Marlene, 'Princess Marie Auguste [of Anhalt]'.
  Royal Musings, 2 January 2010, online,
  http://royalmusingsblogspotcom.blogspot.co.uk/2010/01/princess-
  marie-auguste.html (accessed March 2015)
Miller, Ilana D., 'The very amiables: Henry and Irene of Prussia'.
  In *European Royal History Journal*, LXXIII-LXXV
Van der Kiste, John, ''Poor little insignificant princess': Augusta
  Victoria, the last German Empress'. In *European Royal History
  Journal*, XXVII
Zeepvat, Charlotte, 'Kirche, Küche, Kinder...or perhaps not'. In
  Royalty Digest, Vol. VIII, March and April 1999 (two parts)

Index

of Bismarck, 51; and Boer War, 52-3; and visit to England (1899), 53; dieting, 54; deaths of Duchess Adelaide, Queen Victoria and Empress Frederick, 56-8; love of jewellery, 61; calming effect on husband, 61, 73; daily routine, 62; and court etiquette, 63-4; at wedding of Crown Prince, 65-6; relations with Crown Princess, 66; love of grandchildren, 67; silver wedding anniversary, 67; state visit to Britain 1907, 68-9; and *Daily Telegraph* incident, 72-3; and Emperor's threat to abdicate, 73; and Bulow's resignation, 74; supports the right of women to vote, 74; visit to England 1911, 75; and Moroccan crisis, 76; and Victoria Louise's wedding, 77-8; and William II's silver jubilee, 78-9; and marriage of Oscar, 80-1; and outbreak of World War I, 81-2; wartime work and appeals to German people 83-92; and scandal of Joachim, 87-8; and husband's abdication, 93; leaves for exile in Holland, 93-4; at Amerongen 97-101; at Doorn, in failing health, 102-6; death, 107; funeral, 108-11

ALSO BY JOHN VAN DER KISTE

Royal and historical biography

Frederick III (1981)
Queen Victoria's Family: A Select Bibliography (1982)
Dearest Affie [with Bee Jordaan] (1984)
- revised edition, *Alfred* (2014)
Queen Victoria's Children (1986)
Windsor and Habsburg (1987)
Edward VII's Children (1989)
Princess Victoria Melita (1991)
George V's Children (1991)
George III's Children (1992)
Crowns in a Changing World (1993)
Kings of the Hellenes (1994)
Childhood at Court 1819-1914 (1995)
Northern Crowns (1996)
King George II and Queen Caroline (1997)
The Romanovs 1818-1959 (1998)
Kaiser Wilhelm II (1999)
The Georgian Princesses (2000)
Dearest Vicky, Darling Fritz (2001)
Royal Visits to Devon & Cornwall (2002)
Once a Grand Duchess [with Coryne Hall] (2002)
William and Mary (2003)
Emperor Francis Joseph (2005)
Sons, Servants & Statesmen (2006)
A Divided Kingdom (2007)
William John Wills (2011)
The Prussian Princesses (2014)
The Big Royal Quiz Book (2014)
Prince Henry of Prussia (2015)
Princess Helena (2015)

Local history and true crime

Devon Murders (2006)
Devonshire's Own (2007)
Cornish Murders [with Nicola Sly] (2007)
A Grim Almanac of Devon (2008)
Somerset Murders [with Nicola Sly] (2008)
Cornwall's Own (2008)
Plymouth, History and Guide (2009)
A Grim Almanac of Cornwall (2009)
West Country Murders [with Nicola Sly] (2009)
Jonathan Wild (2009)
Durham Murders & Misdemeanours (2009)
Surrey Murders (2009)
Berkshire Murders (2010)
More Cornish Murders [with Nicola Sly] (2010)
Ivybridge & South Brent Through Time [with Kim Van der Kiste]
   (2010)
Dartmoor from old photographs (2010)
A Grim Almanac of Hampshire (2011)
The Little Book of Devon (2011)
More Devon Murders (2011)
More Somerset Murders [with Nicola Sly] (2011)
The Plymouth Book of Days (2011)
The Little Book of Cornwall (2013)
Plymouth, a City at War 1914-45 (2014)

Music

Roxeventies (1982)
Singles File (1987)
Beyond the Summertime [with Derek Wadeson] (1990)
Gilbert & Sullivan's Christmas (2000)
Roy Wood (2014)
The Little Book of The Beatles (2014)
Jeff Lynne (2015)